Schubert's Theater of Song

Unlocking the Masters Series, No. 17

Schubert's Theater of Song

Mark Ringer

a♭
AMADEUS
PRESS

An Imprint of Hal Leonard Corporation
New York

Published in 2009 by Amadeus Press
An Imprint of Hal Leonard Corporation
7777 West Bluemound Road
Milwaukee, WI 53213

Trade Book Division Editorial Offices
19 West 21st Street, New York, NY 10010

Printed in the United States of America

Book design by Snow Creative Services

Library of Congress Cataloging-in-Publication Data

Ringer, Mark.
  Schubert's theater of song : a listener's guide / Mark Ringer.
     p. cm. -- (Unlocking the masters series ; no. 17)
  Includes bibliographical references and index.
  ISBN 978-1-57467-176-6 (alk. paper)
  1. Schubert, Franz, 1797-1828. Songs. 2. Songs--19th century--Analysis, appreciation.
I. Title.

  ML410.S3R36 2009
  782.42168092--dc22
                              2009008793

www.amadeuspress.com

For Barbara, Deborah, and Lillian

In the short compass of a song, Schubert makes us witness to brief but mortal conflicts.

Franz Liszt

It is a misunderstanding a priori to see in a Lied only a musical miniature with a poetic base. A Schubert Lied contains within itself the essence of all drama and the emotional depth of a cosmic experience.

Dietrich Fischer-Dieskau

Contents

Preface

The Theater of Schubert's Songs

In over six hundred songs composed within a scant eighteen-year career, Franz Schubert created one of the most comprehensive expressions of human experience in any art form. While still in his mid-teens, Schubert was deeply drawn to what was then a marginal musical genre and, almost in an instant, proved it capable of expressing the deepest emotion with the highest level of artistic sophistication. He made the piano-accompanied German song, or *lied*, a major art form while proving himself the greatest songwriter who has ever lived. Art song still suffers under the prejudice of being artificial and "difficult." This is regrettable, since many of music's greatest rewards and pleasures are in this repertoire. Schubert's songs are among the most lovable and profound of all artistic experiences. They rightfully belong to all music lovers, particularly those who value musical drama and the ways music can be united with dramatic or theatrical contexts. The form asks much of its listeners, just as it does of its performers, and consequently many English-speaking listeners may need a guide to help them acclimate to the new terrain. The audience must follow the sung text intently, as one would a Wagner or Monteverdi opera, to understand the musical and dramatic nuances. Many great songs are operas in miniature. The idea of their "small" size is an illusion that disappears once the audience has grasped the song's layers of musical and dramatic meaning. Art songs, Schubert's in particular, often contain more drama than many a full-fledged opera and require performers of exceptional theatrical flair and emotional honesty. Once one has entered Schubert's imaginative world, one's life is forever changed and vistas of feeling and expression open that no other music can replicate.

"Everything exists for its own sake," observed Georg Büchner, the author of *Woyzeck*, political revolutionary, and biologist, shortly before

x   *Preface*

his untimely death at twenty-three years of age in 1837. Büchner's rejection of artificial hierarchies that had dominated the European imagination for centuries can be found also in the unequaled breadth of sympathies expressed in Schubert's songs. Schubert understood and articulated beauty belonging to all human as well as animal and even vegetable existence: from the linden tree to the crow, the happy fisherman, the schizophrenic miller, the contented loner with his cricket, the old man by the winter window, the girl at the spinning wheel, and the cold grip of death itself, who "comes as a friend and not to punish." Nowhere else in music is there a heart as big as this.

My approach to this subject is not as a musicologist but as a teacher, scholar, and practitioner of theater. I hope this perspective will offer fresh insights on Schubert's songs, focusing on their incomparable dramatic power. Ironically, Schubert was, at least during his lifetime, a failed opera composer, often unable to detect when a libretto or its subject was theatrically viable. For Schubert the real "stage" would prove to be not the public theaters of the repressive Austrian regime but the far less censorable theater of song. Schubert's theater of song sprang to life in intimate social gatherings of like-minded friends, wherever a singer and a pianoforte were available. Along with the three great song cycles, *Die Schöne Müllerin* (The Beautiful Girl of the Mill), *Winterreise* (Winter Journey), and *Schwanengesang* (Swan Song), this book will address a range of songs to represent something of Schubert's scope. I also want to shed some light on the poets whose work Schubert chose to set, because they were integral to the song-making process. They were the librettists for whom Schubert had an unfailing sensitivity in his intimate musical theater. This book's structure keeps the idea of the poets in the back of the reader's mind by organizing most chapters according to the poets' nationalities, except in the special cases of Goethe and the great cycles. A few years ago this might have seemed arcane for a general introduction, but the complete Hyperion and the developing Naxos Schubert-Lieder recording series are built in part or almost entirely along such poet-focused lines.

Each song discussion is prefaced by an outline of, or abbreviated passage from, the poem being set to music. The outlines or abbreviations are intended as brief summaries to help orient the reader and not as exact quotations. It is hoped that the listener will have access to the full song texts, which are available in most CD packaging and, increasingly, online.

Many scholars and performers have strongly influenced me. John Reed's encyclopedic *The Schubert Song Companion* is an essential reference for anyone with an interest in this repertoire. The fine translations of Richard Stokes and Richard Wigmore are invaluable for English-language readers. Elizabeth Norman McKay, Brian Newbould, Rita Steblin, and Susan Youens's work has helped bring Schubert's milieu and Biedermeier culture into sharper focus. The accompanist Graham Johnson has not only recorded each Schubert song but also created fascinating and comprehensive annotations for his Hyperion series. Finally, the baritone Dietrich Fischer-Dieskau's pioneering work as a concert and recording artist, not to mention his own writing on Schubert, makes him the artistic, intellectual, and spiritual guide who continues to lead the majority of people to the universe of Schubert's lieder.

I wish to thank my wonderful editor and friend, Robert Levine, for his belief in this project, as well as the staff of Amadeus Press. I am grateful for the Senior Fellowship Leave I was granted by Marymount Manhattan College and the generous support from the estate of Margaret Sokol that helped make the writing of this book possible. The generosity, insight, and kindness of Frau Dietlinde Rakowitz made a visit to the Schloss Atzenbrugg Schubert-Gedenkstätte und Museum a moving and unforgettable experience. I have been greatly encouraged by Professors Mary Fleischer, William J. Bordeau, Richard Niles, Haila Strauss, and Tibor Farkas, as well as Deans Dawn Weber and Peter Baker. I also wish to thank Vice President Maureen Grant and President Judson Shaver of Marymount Manhattan College. Friends like Mira Felner, Richard and Joshua Cutler, Inge Walther, Carol Cantrell, Lisa Haage, Denise Field, Donna Ellis, Jon Mullich, Steve Mack, Charles Richards, Bruce Lazarus, Brian Hurley, and Jeff Joneikis have always been there to lend support, share a laugh, or talk music. An old colleague, the late singer and writer Robert Prag, taught me that there are many equally valid ways to sing a song. More recently, Rinaldo Petronio has afforded me insights in conversation that have resonated in my explorations of these great songs.

My wife, Barbara Bosch, is my truest inspiration, and her belief in me helps me over all the rough patches. As always, Deborah Bosch and Lillian Bosch provided priceless technological and moral support. My belief that Schubert's death at thirty-one is the single greatest loss in the history of art was fostered by my late father, Gordon Ringer. I owe my love of lieder to my late mother, Dr. Virginia Hartt Ringer, professor of philosophy. She had studied singing before she discovered she loved philosophy even more. She had learned many lieder and, on the advice of an old friend named Vico Palmieri, sang me Brahms's "Lullaby" and other songs in German when I was still a babe in arms so that I'd "love lieder" when I got older. Vico's idea of German "Kultur" was far from romanticized; he was a half Jew who had bitterly fought the German army in Greece during the war against Nazism, but he knew that art is what remains when everything else is forgotten and that no language sounds better than German when it is well sung. The stratagem worked.

Schubert's Theater of Song

What Is a Lied?

S ome definitions are in order. An art song is a classical composition involving a solo singer and a piano accompanist. It is sometimes said that art songs are what opera singers perform when they are "off duty" from the opera house. There is some truth to this. Almost all important opera singers perform concerts apart from their operatic work. Often in such recitals, especially when they are accompanied by a piano rather than an orchestra, they may perform both songs and opera arias. Most opera singers have at least some experience with art songs even if they only perform a few. In addition to opera singers, every generation has singers of international repute who specialize in art song. Like opera, this genre demands strong musical and dramatic sensibility. Singers of art songs, however, have only a few minutes at most to establish the character they are playing or the story they are relating, the setting and atmosphere of the song's dramatic situation. With only a piano to back them up, the concentration upon the singers becomes all enveloping. After all, the singers are stripped of makeup, costume, setting, and the dozens of other distractions that are part of a staged opera. Their gestures and bodily movements are similarly constrained to focus attention on the song.

The singers of art songs have nothing to hide behind. They address their audience directly, just as actors performed soliloquies in the theater of Shakespeare's time. When it all works, a rapport is created with the audience of exceptional intimacy. In the more seriously conceived art songs the pianist becomes the equal partner of the vocalist. Sometimes the keyboard writing demands from the pianist an even greater responsibility for the creation of the musical/dramatic situation.

It is ideal that the singer and accompanist share a close musical and emotional sympathy. Together they create an intimate theater of song.

The first building block of the art song is the text, usually derived from the lyric poetry tradition of the composer's homeland. Art song traditions have flourished all over the Western world, but the countries most instrumental to their development have been Austria and Germany. There, the piano-accompanied song, or *lied* (the plural is *lieder*), arrived during the later decades of the eighteenth century. The cataclysm of the Thirty Years' War had left Germany culturally ravaged for generations. Only in the mid-eighteenth century was a significant lyric poetry tradition established that would serve as impetus for serious songwriting. Amateur music making, from singing to instrument playing, reached very high standards, particularly in great urban centers like Vienna and Berlin. The rapid development and overwhelming popularity of the pianoforte, able to create a near-orchestral range of sounds within the confines of a nobleman's salon or a middle-class drawing room, encouraged composers to write more challenging accompaniments to their songs.

The great composers of the Viennese classical tradition, Haydn, Mozart, and Beethoven, created important lieder, but the form was never a central concern for any of them. Nevertheless, several songs of Mozart and Beethoven in particular give a clear idea of the form's possibilities when the vocal part unites with an equally important piano accompaniment. In his song "Das Veilchen" (The Little Violet) of 1785, Mozart sets a poem about a little flower that symbolizes the fragility of innocence with a lovely vocal melody that fits the narrative and mood of the words. The piano part gives the song an extra sense of atmosphere, occasionally adding musical commentary apart from the voice, just as Mozart does with his orchestral accompaniments in his operas. Mozart's song becomes a kind of vocal chamber music that transforms a lyric poem into a minioperatic scene. Within another generation Beethoven would prove the lied capable of sustained musical development with his song cycle *An die ferne Geliebte* (To the Distant Beloved) of 1816. A group of six songs tell a continuous story, with the composer linking them through the piano accompaniment into a composition lasting a quarter of an hour.

Already by the late eighteenth century, the general structural patterns of lied composition were being used. Some lieder are called strophic songs, meaning that each verse or strophe of the poem is set to exactly the same vocal and keyboard music. The challenge for the composer is to create music that is equally appropriate for each verse, a true musical distillation of the poem. A modified strophic song is, as the name implies, a strophic song with some, usually minimal, alteration of the musical materials from verse to verse. A through-composed or *durchkomponiert* song is one where virtually each verse is treated to different music to bring out all the changing elements in the poem. This style of construction challenges the composer to create unity in diversity, manipulating often strongly contrasting musical material into a coherent whole. Like opera, lieder sometimes embrace passages of recitative, the speech-song declamation that moves operatic action forward. Oftentimes these recitative sections utilize snippets of melody or arioso passages to contrast with the recitative. Frequently these ariosos are elaborated into more fully fledged arialike writing. During his brief career, Schubert created lieder using all of the constructive techniques mentioned above, illuminating a path for generations of future lieder composers all the way to Mahler and Strauss in the twentieth century.

But for all the great lieder composers who followed Schubert, his songs stand unique and inimitable. As Leo Black observes:

> Here expression and [tone] painting can no longer even be separated: what man sings, he is . . . : one hears a great Schubert song and immediately feels the man himself is there before or even within one. "Primitive" peoples, such as the Australian aborigines, firmly believe the world holds no danger so long as one can sing the right tune. Strange though it may sound, the Biedermeier, mushroom-like figure of Franz Peter Schubert concealed an ancestor of that kind, for whom there is identity not merely between feeling and painting, but between what is painted and what is felt. (Black 1997, 27)

Schubert's Life

As with many great artists, people have tried to reduce the full stature of Schubert by affixing labels to him that seemed adequate at the time but have since proven limiting. During his life some of his friends affectionately nicknamed him "*Schwammerl*," "little mushroom," i.e., "tubby," hardly a dignified appellation for the only musician whose natural talent came closest to Mozart's. He has been labeled a miniaturist, a master of lieder and impromptus but inept at larger forms. The popularization of his major instrumental works, with their unprecedented breadth of vision directly pointing the way to Bruckner and Mahler, has largely dashed this idea. Perhaps the biggest howler is Grillparzer's notorious epitaph: "Here the art of music has buried a rich treasure but far more beautiful hopes." As Alfred Brendel has frequently pointed out, death certainly robbed us of many masterpieces when it took Schubert at age thirty-one, but works "more beautiful" than *Winterreise*, the String Quintet, and the B-flat Major Piano Sonata simply could not exist. One of my own favorite bits of reductionism is found in Richard Cappel's otherwise beautiful book of 1928, *Schubert's Songs*. He offers the blanket characterization of Schubert as one "who knew nothing but the rapture and poignancy of first sensations, the loss of which is the beginning of wisdom" (1). Cappel himself provides many examples that show how wrong-headed this infantilizing generalization is, yet his uncharacteristically silly remark is still quoted reverently. Schubert always surprises us, just as he did his contemporaries. Like life itself, he cannot be pinned down.

Schubert and his circle lived much of their lives under the shadow of Napoleonic invasion and, after that threat was removed, the forbidding conditions of a police state. With the end of the Napoleonic Wars in 1815 Austria settled into a reactionary regime ruled by the Emperor Franz I and his right-hand man, the state chancellor, Prince Clemens Metternich. Speech and the press were heavily censored. The government depended on a network of spies. Innocent people could be arrested and held without trial. The average Austrian settled with necessity by creating a kind of nineteenth-century cocooning we now call the Biedermeier era. The term *Biedermeier* was originally a humorous combination of two words. *Bieder* meant "honest, upright, but also ordinary" and *Meier* was an Austrian family name as ubiquitous as "Smith" is in the English-speaking world today (Erickson 1997, 33 fn. 17). Putting them together, this neologism embodied the art and culture of middle-class German-speaking Europe between the fall of Napoleon and the revolutions of 1848. The ideal Biedermeier citizen was scrupulously apolitical, focused on familial and domestic pleasures. But many found Metternich's tyranny unbearable. During Schubert's creative life, suicide and attempted suicide were only too common (Fischer-Dieskau 1978, 104). As will be seen throughout this book, Schubert's art is as paradoxically complex in its acceptance of and rebellion against Biedermeier culture as Shostakovich's music is in relation to the culture of the Soviet Union.

Schubert's parents came from the northern extremes of the Austro-Hungarian empire. His father, Franz Theodor Florian Schubert, was a schoolmaster from Moravia and his mother, Maria Elisabeth Katherina Vietz, was a domestic servant from Silesia. They met and married in Vienna. Of their twelve children, only four survived to adulthood. Franz Peter Schubert was born on January 31, 1797 in the family's apartment, in a building that still stands and serves as a Schubert museum. The Schuberts were a very musical family. Franz was taught the violin by his father and the piano by his brother Ignaz. The composer's earliest string quartets, disarmingly charming works, were created for family music making. Franz's extraordinary musical aptitude was spotted early and encouraged by his father, who sent him to study with the choirmaster of their local church, Michael Holzer, who, according to the composer's father, "averred again and again, with tears in his eyes, that he had never had such a pupil. 'If I wanted to teach him something new,' he used to say, 'he already knew it. Consequently I gave him no real instruction but merely talked with him and regarded him with silent astonishment'" (Deutsch 1958, 212). All was well so long as the boy kept a realistic perspective that joining the family "business" at the schoolhouse would be his ultimate career and music reserved as a pastime for idle hours. This assumption would sow the seeds for familial conflict in the future.

In 1808 Franz became a student at the Imperial and Royal City College (the Stadtkonvikt) and a member of its imperial boys' choir, in which the young Haydn had once performed and that survives today as the Vienna Boys' Choir. The Stadtkonvikt was "the select and strict school for non-noble boys closely connected to the court; his acceptance indicates that Schubert was recognized from the start as having special potential" (Erickson 1997, 16). The Stadtkonvikt training formed the backbone of much of Schubert's musical, intellectual, and social life. The choir introduced him to many great choral works of the past. The school orchestra familiarized him with symphonies of the classical tradition. His exceptional musical gifts were encouraged by his teachers, who allowed him time to study privately with the aging master teacher, Antonio Salieri. Salieri, we are now learning through revivals of his operas and a CD dedicated to his works sung by Cecilia Bartoli, was a fine composer. He has been unfairly (however entertainingly) maligned for centuries by the likes of Pushkin, Rimsky-Korsakov, and most recently Peter Shaffer in his play and film *Amadeus* as the "patron saint of mediocrity" and the enemy of real talent. This was certainly not Schubert's experience with the old master, with whom he shared a mutually affectionate relationship for the several years he studied with him.

Salieri, true to his proud Italian heritage, encouraged Schubert to master the art of setting Italian verses to music. For Salieri, German was hardly the language for music, nor could the old man see much point in composing German songs, one of his brilliant student's increasing preoccupations. Salieri impressed upon Schubert the necessity of becoming a successful opera composer to ensure a decent living in a precarious profession. Schubert would diligently seek operatic success throughout his professional life. Unlike all the other musical genres that he made entirely his own, Schubert's many operatic works remain on the periphery of the repertoire. Composers such as Cavalli, Vivaldi, and Handel have had to languish far longer for a modern reevaluation in the operatic theater, and perhaps a similar fate awaits Schubert's work in this field. His fascinating fragmentary cantata, *Lazarus*, composed in 1820, anticipates the style of Wagner's *Lohengrin* by several decades and may hint at the kind of music drama Schubert might have developed had he lived longer. Fortunately, Schubert's miraculous creativity in all other compositional forms makes such speculation seem a symptom of ingratitude.

It was during his time at the college that Schubert began forming the network of friends that would sustain him throughout his life. He met Josef von Spaun, nine years his senior, while both were rehearsing with the school orchestra. Spaun would introduce him to many of Schubert's most important friends, including Franz von Schober, Johann Mayrhofer, and Moriz von Schwind. These friends, along with their families and other acquaintances, would make up the nucleus of the future Schubertiads, the legendary semi-impromptu drawing-room gatherings in which Schubert would demonstrate his newest compositions and often improvise dances for hours on end. Spaun would help the composer throughout his life, disseminating his music whenever his civil service work necessitated travel through Austria. He also carefully maintained manuscripts and provided biographical information after Schubert's death, which helped the composer's posthumous reputation.

In 1812, when he was fifteen years old, Schubert's mother died. This was a major turning point in his life, as it would be for anyone. This experience may well have informed his lifelong obsession with death, which was well established long before the onset of his own chronic illness. In virtually all of Schubert's music, death is simultaneously terrifying and consoling, as in the song "Der Tod und das Mädchen" (Death and the Maiden; see Chapter 4). Schubert's imagination sees death as the central duality in an existence made up of dualities. Schubert's father remarried the next year, and the composer enjoyed a warm relationship with his stepmother, Anna Kleyenböck. Schubert entered the family profession in 1814, teaching at his father's school. This move may have had as much to do with avoiding military conscription as with bowing to paternal pressure. Schubert hated teaching, and occasionally took out his frustrations on his students with his cane when they interrupted his attempts at composition in the classroom. Years later, an affair with one of his former female charges ended with her dumping him because she could not reconcile herself to his earlier cruelties. "It is quite true," Schubert complained to a friend, "whenever I was composing, this little gang annoyed me so much that the ideas always went out of my head. Naturally I gave them a good hiding then—and now I have to suffer for it!" (Deutsch 1958, 202). For all the unpleasantness of his day job, this also happened to be the year of his first compositional breakthrough, the creation of the first great lied, a setting of Goethe's poem "Gretchen am Spinnrade." He was only seventeen years old. Soon "Gretchen" would be joined by the equally important Goethe setting of "Erlkönig."

This year saw also the creation of his first mass for soloists, chorus, and orchestra (in F major, D. 105; D numbers refer to the scholar Otto Erich Deutsch's chronological catalogue of Schubert's works), which he successfully conducted in a performance at the family's parish church. The soprano soloist, Therese Grob, almost two years younger than the composer, sang his music beautifully. She had "a heart of gold," Schubert later observed, and he fell deeply in love with her. Many songs he wrote during the next two years were designed specifically for her bright soprano voice. The years 1815 and 1816, while the Grob relationship was at its height, were, not coincidentally, the most musically productive period in Schubert's life, including the composition of 254 songs. Schubert hoped to marry Therese, but his poor salary as a schoolmaster—he never developed talent at selling his music—forced a termination of the relationship. Under the oppressive marriage laws of the time, a potential bridegroom had to prove a large enough income to be allowed by the state to marry and start a family. Schubert never forgot Therese, even after her family pressured her into marrying a wealthy baker in 1820. The bitterness of this loss and the naturally ensuing sexual frustration would, in a few years' time, lead Schubert into the reckless behavior that brought about his deadly illness.

Schubert's emotional and creative frustrations led eventually to a brief but bitter break with his father. With the help of his friend Franz von Schober, Schubert renounced the schoolhouse for good. Schober was Schubert's closest friend and undoubtedly his most controversial one; some members of their circle would blame him for leading Schubert into self-destructive behavior. Schober was a handsome, wealthy aristocrat with a penchant for womanizing and artistic dilettantism; he stood for everything that Schubert was not (Deutsch 1958, 87). This undoubtedly made him an attractive figure to the socially awkward composer, whose musical genius in turn made him an attractive friend for Schober. What did Schober get from the relationship? Immortality. Schubert set several of his friend's verses as great lieder and Schober provided the libretto for the first of Schubert's mature full-length operas, *Alfonso und Estrella* (1821–22).

By 1817 the composer had moved in with Schober and his mother, which helped Schubert shake off the stifling parochialism of his father's house. Schober made it possible for Schubert to realize his dream of independence to pursue his art. This setup also created a model for many of the composer's living arrangements over the years; he lodged with friends when he could not afford to live independently. Most important of all, Schober arranged for Schubert to meet one of his artistic idols, the star baritone Johann Michael Vogl, who had created the role of Pizarro in the 1814 premiere of Beethoven's *Fidelio*. Vogl, a great singing actor in the twilight of his stage career, almost immediately perceived the genius of Schubert's songs and dedicated the rest of his long life to performing them. Vogl led Schubert on the world's first lieder recital tours in 1819, 1823, and 1825 through the singer's native upper Austria. He proved a "second father" to the composer, offering considerable financial and artistic support (Deutsch 1958, 14). Another important friend in these years of transition was Johann Baptist Mayrhofer. Schubert shared lodgings with him between 1818 and 1820. Mayrhofer was a civil servant who had a genuine poetic talent, and Schubert set more of his poetry than anyone else's except Goethe and Schiller. Mayrhofer, like the singer Vogl, was a passionate lover of the Greek and Latin classics, and this influenced Schubert until he broke free from his severely depressive friend, not without a considerable cooling of their friendship.

This is as good a moment as any to address the issue of sexuality, which has dominated so much American Schubert scholarship since the 1980s. Like any human being, Schubert could have been gay or bisexual, and would have had for company many of the greatest artists and human beings who have ever lived, but all the evidence points stubbornly in the other direction. The historical documentation of his short life provides ample evidence of Schubert's heterosexuality and that of virtually all of his male friends, but the enduring nineteenth-century cliché that his music is somehow "feminine" in comparison to that of the more ostensibly "masculine" Beethoven, as well as the linkage between sexuality and mortality in Schubert's life, which has such obvious parallels with the AIDS crisis emerging in the 1980s, led some musicologists to attempt, often with great ingenuity, to "out" the composer. A "conspiracy" to hide the truth of Schubert's sexual orientation has been posited that in its breadth nearly rivals the convoluted, counterintuitive claims of proponents of the "Shakespeare authorship question." The work of the musicologist Rita Steblin (1993) effectively exploded the "gay" theory for any sensible researcher, but American academic identity politics makes it difficult to let it go. Valuable biographical research is often jettisoned in favor of fanciful speculation and many scholars politely submit to the ideology of the moment out of fear of being branded homophobic. It is to be hoped that the coming years will see an abandonment of this intellectual cul-de-sac when a new generation of scholars reads the biographical documentation afresh and utilizes common sense.

From 1818 to 1822, Schubert made both small and major breakthroughs. As always, his song composing continued unabated. He enjoyed a stint as music master for a branch of the Esterházy family (Haydn's patrons) on their Hungarian estate at Zselíz for several months in 1818. His principal task was the musical instruction of the count's two little girls. He was well treated by the family and heard gypsy and other Eastern European music, which haunted his imagination for the rest of his life. He also found time for an affair with the countess's chambermaid, Josefine "Pepi" Pöckelhofer (Schubert 1970, 45; Deutsch 1958, 100, 104; Steblin 2008). Within a year he would write the first of his piano sonatas to enter the permanent repertoire (the A major, Op. 120) and the "Trout" Quintet, one of the world's most beloved chamber works. Early in 1821, Vogl gave the first public performance

of Schubert's "Erlkönig" at Vienna's Kärntnertor Theater, which had to
be encored. Clive observes that Vogl's "performance that day undoubtedly helped to establish Schubert's reputation as an exceptionally gifted
song composer outside the more limited circle of music lovers who had
already come to admire him at private gatherings" (1997, 248). Only
one month later, a group of Schubert's friends pooled their resources
to have "Erlkönig" privately published to great success, alerting the
reticent publishing houses to Schubert's commercial viability. His professional career was finally getting under way. He must have felt himself
closing in on the elusive operatic career he'd dreamed of when his comic
operetta, *Die Zwillingsbrüder* (The Twin Brothers), tailored for Michael
Vogl's talents, enjoyed a modest success. This would remain, however,
the only one of his operatic works to be staged in his lifetime.

By the year 1822, Schubert had reached an exciting new stage in his
mastery of larger forms. He was drafting a symphony in the unusual
key of B minor (the "Unfinished") that broke new ground both structurally and expressively, ushering a new world of romantic subjectivity
into symphonic writing. For unknown reasons his inspiration appears
to have dried up after he completed the first two movements and the
opening fragment of a scherzo. This is also the time of the so-called
"Wanderer" Fantasy, Op. 15, his most virtuosic piano work. Based
on a theme from one of his most popular songs, "Der Wanderer" (see
Chapter 4), the fantasy is a tour de force of monothematicism in which
all four movements are linked, creating a vision of organic unity that
many romantic composers would struggle to emulate. His songs were
the subject of frequent positive critical notice throughout the German-
language press. One important Viennese critic declared in March 1822,
"Schubert's songs raise themselves by ever undeniable excellences to
the rank of masterpieces of genius, calculated to restore the present
debased taste; for never has the true force of genius failed in its effect
on heart and mind" (Deutsch 1977, 214). A month after this review,
Schubert made a personal approach to Beethoven himself, securing the
older master's permission to dedicate to him a set of piano four-hands
variations (in E minor, D. 624). By August, it is reported, Beethoven
had exclaimed of Schubert, "This one will surpass me" (Deutsch 1977,
232)—which disproves the legend that Beethoven was unaware of his

younger colleague until the older man was on his deathbed! Schubert may have been relatively poor all his life, creating dozens of masterpieces that would have to wait decades before their public performance, but by 1822 he was becoming famous in Vienna on the strength of his songs alone.

But in early 1823 irreparable disaster struck, as Schubert was hospitalized with the symptoms of syphilis, presumably caught from a prostitute on one of his forays into Vienna's brothels. (Later in the century, Brahms too would prove addicted to visiting prostitutes but would enjoy far better luck in this regard.) Schubert now knew his time was probably drastically limited. Syphilis is an insidious disease that can lurk dormant for long periods of time, allowing its victims a false sense of security before erupting in ugly lesions, rashes, and debilitating headaches. In the world before penicillin, "treatment" consisted of exposure to mercury, which was agonizing, poisonous, and little more than a palliative. In the final stage, the illness often assaults the central nervous system and causes dementia. The five years of life remaining to him would include periods of seeming remission interrupted by the resurfacing of the disease and his enforced retreat into his lodgings for prolonged periods of time. Considering Biedermeier attitudes toward sexuality, Schubert's deadly illness was doubtless exacerbated by the moral revulsion of "decent" society, much as victims of AIDS have experienced in our supposedly more enlightened times. In August 1823 Beethoven's nephew wrote in one of his uncle's conversation books, "They greatly praise Schubert, but it is said that he hides himself" (Deutsch 1977, 288). Like Beethoven's deafness, Schubert's illness would serve as both the curse of his existence and the driving, differentiating fact of his life. It would color all his later works and allow him unprecedented insight into the suffering of humankind. Within the first year of his illness Schubert remarked: "Pain sharpens the understanding and strengthens the mind; whereas joy seldom troubles about the former and softens the latter or makes it frivolous" (Deutsch 1977, 336). Schubert "Composer of first sensations" indeed!

The probability that his life would be shortened led Schubert to a work regimen that seems almost superhuman. Even during his first hospitalization he began work on one of his most original masterpieces, the song cycle *Die Schöne Müllerin*. His A Minor Piano Sonata, D. 784, a work of "deadly earnestness" (Brendel 2007), is another product of this sad time. In 1823 he composed his last two completed operas, *Fierrabras* and *Die Verschworenen* (The Conspirators), each created with a reasonable expectation of production that failed to materialize. Dauntless in the face of all the year's appalling professional and physical setbacks, Schubert wrote critically praised incidental music for a flop play, *Rosamunde*, as well several of his most beautiful songs, including "Du bist die Ruh" and "Auf dem Wasser zu singen" (see Chapter 4). By the summer he had recovered enough to join Vogl on a working vacation to upper Austria, though he became "seriously ill" in Vogl's hometown of Steyr (Deutsch 1977, 296).

Schubert's friends would frequently attempt to cheer him and each other by expressing belief in his "recovery," and it is likely that given the nature of the disease, the composer was very selective about those to whom he revealed the truth. One such friend was the painter Leopold Kupelwieser, to whom he addressed the most famous and harrowing of his surviving letters, dated March 31, 1824.

> At last I can wholly pour out my whole heart to someone again. You are so good and faithful, you are sure to forgive me things that others would only take very much amiss. —To be brief, I feel myself to be the most unfortunate and the most wretched man in the whole world. Picture to yourself someone whose health is permanently injured, and who, in sheer despair, does everything to make it worse instead of better; picture to yourself, I say, someone whose most brilliant hopes have come to nothing, someone to whom love and friendship are at most a source of bitterness, someone whose inspiration (whose creative inspiration at least) for all that is beautiful threatens to fail, and then ask yourself if that is not a wretched and unhappy being. "My peace is gone, my heart is sore, I shall find it never and nevermore." That could be my daily song now, for every night when I go to sleep I hope never to wake again, and each morning I am only recalled to the griefs of yesterday.

The quoted refrain is from his first great song, "Gretchen am Spinnrade." It is typical of Schubert that along with pouring out his

heart, he mentions that he has just completed three chamber mas-
terpieces: the A Minor and D Minor String Quartets, as well as his
Octet for Winds and Strings to "prepare the way for a big symphony"
(Schubert 1970, 77–80).

That summer brought seemingly better health and a return to
the Esterházy estate in Zselíz as music master for the maturing children. This must have been one of the most bittersweet experiences of
Schubert's life, as he came in contact with this family again under the
shadow of his (to them certainly) secret illness. The affair with the
chambermaid had run its course. During this stay, Schubert developed
a powerful attachment to the eldest daughter, Caroline Esterházy, now
a young woman. The social differences alone made her utterly unattainable. This idealized love sustained the composer during his last
years. Many years later, Countess Caroline's portrait was significantly
placed in the background by Schubert's friend, the painter Moritz
von Schwind, in his iconic drawing "Schubert Evening at Joseph von
Spaun's," signaling the countess's emotional importance to the composer. She once teased Schubert for never dedicating any of his works
to her. "What is the point? Everything is dedicated to you anyway," he
is supposed to have replied, with surprising candor for so shy a man
(Deutsch 1958, 100). Schubert may, however, have continued to seek
out less platonic female companionship in spite of the risk of spreading
his infection. One acquaintance writes of seeing "Schubert with his girl"
at a new-wine inn during 1827. "He came to join us and did not show
himself again" (Deutsch 1977, 658–59). As one scholar observes: "It is
for the reader's own informed understanding and imagination to draw
what conclusions it will" (Newbould 1997, 260).

The summer and fall of 1825 marked the happiest time of Schubert's
later years as he went on an extended concert tour with Vogl through
upper Austria. Their lieder performances set the standard for what the
world now expects of the genre. He wrote his brother Ferdinand, "The
way in which Vogl sings and I accompany him, so that we seem to be
fused for the moment into a single being, is something entirely new and
unknown to these people" (Schubert 1970, 105). It was on this trip,
with its inspiring natural scenery, that Schubert composed "Ave Maria"
(see Chapter 6), "Die Allmacht" (see Chapter 5), the D Major Piano

Sonata, and the Great C Major Symphony. Two of the most revealing letters regarding Schubert's personality derive from this trip. While detailing to his parents the matchless scenery of upper Austria, Schubert gently teases his hypochondriac brother, Ferdinand.

> He has doubtless been ill 77 times again, and has thought 9 times that he was going to die, as though dying were the worst that can happen to a man! If only he could once see these heavenly mountains and lakes, the sight of which threatens to crush or engulf us, he would not be so attached to puny human life, nor regard it otherwise than good fortune to be confided to earth's indescribable power of creating new life. (Deutsch 1977, 436)

Schubert's Linz friend Anton Ottenwalt reported to Spaun a late-evening discussion with the composer.

> We sat together until not far from midnight, and I have never seen him like this, nor heard: serious, profound and as though inspired. How he talked of art, of poetry, of his youth, of friends and other people who matter, of the relationship of ideals to life, &c.! I was more and more amazed at such a mind, of which it has been said that its artistic achievement is so unconscious, hardly revealed to and understood by himself, and so on. Yet how simple was all this! —I cannot tell you of the extent and unity of his convictions—but there were glimpses of a world-view that is not merely acquired, and the share which worthy friends may have in it by no means detracts from the individuality shown by all this. (Deutsch 1977, 442)

1826 saw the creation of two visionary masterpieces in G major, the Piano Sonata, Op. 78 and the last of the String Quartets, D. 887, along with many fine songs. The most important composition of 1827 was surely Schubert's setting of the *Winterreise* cycle by Wilhelm Müller, the same poet whose *Die Schöne Müllerin* poetry had so inspired him four years before. *Winterreise* is unquestionably the greatest song cycle ever written and may even represent Schubert's highest achievement as a composer. The work took months and, if we are to believe the recollections of his friends, cost him more intellectual and spiritual capital than any other. By March of 1827 Beethoven was dead, and Schubert served as a torchbearer at his funeral. Schubert was aware that he now bore the mantle of the older master, and he would not waste any of whatever time was left to prove himself worthy of it.

The period between Beethoven's death and Schubert's in November of the following year was, in the opinion of the British composer Benjamin Britten, the most productive year and a half in the history of music. In March 1828 Schubert organized the only concert given in his lifetime made up entirely of his own compositions. It was a success, and more such events would have surely followed had he lived longer. In a period of feverish creativity, Schubert completed the last and greatest of his masses and the final three piano sonatas, which mark the apex of the form along with Beethoven's final three. He created several of his most popular short pieces for piano and wrote the F Minor Fantasy for piano four hands, the greatest work in the history of this medium, which he dedicated to Countess Caroline Esterházy. His C Major Fantasy for violin and piano is one of the masterpieces for that instrumental combination and deserves to be better known. His C Major String Quintet from his final weeks is widely regarded, with Beethoven's late quartets, as the highest achievement in chamber music. Along with revisions on the Great C Major Symphony, Schubert sketched a "Tenth" Symphony in D Major that lay undiscovered until 1978. Its orchestral realization and performance reveal the beginnings of a masterpiece that clearly anticipates the work of Mahler.

He also found time for individual lieder as well as a group of fourteen songs, which would be published posthumously as a song cycle, *Schwanengesang*. The high productivity and consistent greatness of Schubert's music of 1828 boggle the imagination. His final illness, probably typhus assaulting his critically weakened metabolism, was mercifully quick and took his friends and family by surprise. He died on November 19, 1828 while being nursed in his brother Ferdinand's apartment. Some of his last words uttered in a state of delirium were "Beethoven does not lie here" (Deutsch 1977, 825). Ferdinand interpreted this as a wish to be buried near his great hero, and, as we can now appreciate, his artistic equal. Schubert's and Beethoven's graves were moved during the late 1800s but are still adjacent each other in Vienna's Zentralfriedhoff, honoring Schubert's wishes. Schwind, his painter friend, wrote to Schober, "The more I realize now what he was like, the more I see what he has suffered" (Deutsch 1977, 829).

Most of the composer's music was unpublished during his lifetime. Even his closest friends, although they had long understood his greatness as a song composer, had no inkling of his achievements in instrumental music. Indeed, Schubert's position as the "Prince of Song" was solidified by his mid-twenties and has never been seriously challenged since. His other works took longer to find acceptance, due in large measure to their extraordinary innovative aspects. The first more or less complete edition of Schubert's works would only appear at the end of the nineteenth century, giving the world an idea of the composer's almost inconceivable scope. The twentieth century saw many performers, from Dietrich Fischer-Dieskau to Artur Schnabel, the Busch Quartet, and Alfred Brendel, whose advocacy of Schubert's music has led to his current position as one of the very greatest of the world's great composers, a master of every form he attempted, except perhaps opera. But in Schubert's theater of song he reigned as a supreme dramatist, the greatest the world of song has ever known.

Robert Schumann observed soon after Schubert's death, "Schubert's music is as varied as the thousand shapes of mankind's thoughts and aspirations" (qtd. in Fischer-Dieskau, 290). The German mezzo Brigitte Fassbaender, arguably the most personal and original of Schubert's modern interpreters, had the courage to express what many feel about this reclusive, painfully shy man who died nearly two centuries ago, a few months short of his thirty-second birthday. "The humanity, modernity and depth of Schubert's musical testimony makes him the most brilliant of all brilliant composers: immortal, indelible, inexplicable" (1997, 12).

Goethe Settings

Schubert's empathy with Goethe's lyric poetry is the foundation of European art song. As Fischer-Dieskau observes, "No poet so fired Schubert's creative imagination as did Goethe. Everything that Schubert strove to express in music, clarity of thought and expression, deep emotion, imaginative language, all this he found in Goethe's poetry. Here he was confronted with that unity of Art and Nature which was part of his own personality" 1978, 52). By the 1770s, Johann Wolfgang von Goethe (1749–1832) had established himself as the greatest poet and writer in the German language. Goethe's "collaboration" with Schubert, as so often in the world of lieder, was one sided. Schubert made two attempts over the years to contact Goethe in Weimar, where the old poet was regarded as the supreme European man of letters. A public endorsement from Goethe would have opened many doors for Schubert. Unfortunately, Goethe's musical tastes were extremely conservative and strongly influenced by his close friend, the composer Carl Friederich Zelter. Zelter was a fine music teacher distinguished for having trained the young Mendelssohn. But Zelter was no friend of Schubert's kind of compositional innovation. Schubert's scores were returned by Goethe without comment. The Schubert Goethe settings, seventy-four in all, are now regarded as one of the greatest collections of songs created by a composer from the works of a single poet and are the principal means by which Goethe's name is kept alive outside of German-speaking countries.

"Gretchen am Spinnrade" (Gretchen at the Spinning Wheel), D. 118 (1814) (CD Track 1)

> *Gretchen is the innocent country girl seduced and ultimately*
> *destroyed by Faust in Goethe's most famous play. "My peace is gone,*
> *my heart is heavy. My mind is shattered. The flow of his words, his*
> *hand in mine, and ah, his kiss! I want to die under his kisses!"*

On October 19, 1814, the seventeen-year-old Schubert completed this
song and with it virtually invented a new musical genre. The vocal writing projects the psychology of the character with a vividness matched
only by the greatest opera composers. The piano's role radically and
forever altered its position from mere harmonic and generalized support
for the singer to active partner: the singer's "setting," her mood, her
alter ego, an articulation of her subconscious long before Freud gave
the world this theoretical construct.

The girl's spinning wheel is literally conjured before us with unprecedented boldness by the pianist's whirling notes. But more engaging still
is the way the concrete image of the spinning wheel so easily doubles
as a metaphor for the confused emotions whirling within her mind,
stirred by her newly awakened sexuality. As the music builds (0:35),
one can tell Gretchen is losing not only composure but also her control
of the spinning wheel. At the climactic "And, ah, his kiss" (Und ach,
sein Kuss!; 1:45), which sends her voice to its highest point in the song,
the piano is silenced for a breathless, frightening moment (1:52). Slowly
Gretchen gathers her resources. After a tentative start (1:55), the flow
of the spinning wheel resumes (2:02). The song's opening words are
repeated, only to mark the beginning of a new crisis as she imagines
grabbing hold of Faust and "dying from his kisses" (An seinen Küssen /
Vergehen sollt'!; 2:40) The musical repetitions, suggesting her obsession, lead her to another breaking point (3:01). Schubert ends the song
with her exhausted reiteration of "My peace is gone, my heart is heavy"
(Meine Ruh ist hin, / Mein Herz ist schwer; 3:05). These words sound
the depths of a broken, exhausted soul.

Whenever the song is effectively performed, a rare silence possesses
the space. For a teacher it is a privilege to watch students' faces when

they are introduced to this work. One sees what the teenage Schubert saw in the eyes of his young friends as his imagination conjured forth a new world of expressive possibility. Schubert's spirit seems to physically enter the room, manifest in the song's genuinely unnerving emotional depth. How a teenage boy could have created a work of such perfectly assured form, containing such radical stylistic innovation and such emotional maturity, is one of the great mysteries of the world.

"Meeres Stille" (Quiet Sea), D. 216 (1815)

> *"Deep stillness reigns on the water, and the nervous sailor looks at the sea's glassy surface."*

Schubert created his quietest and yet most terrifying "water music" to set Goethe's words. It is marked "Very slow, anxious." One must look ahead generations, to the works of the impressionists, for music resembling Schubert's vision of the sea's threatening stasis. This is word painting of a boldness whose only antecedents may be found in Bach's vocal works and Monteverdi's most radically experimental music in the early seventeenth century. (Baroque enthusiasts may recall the Italian master's famous "Or che'l ciel e la terra" from the *Eighth Book of Madrigals*.) Fischer-Dieskau writes, "The score of the song looks like a drawing, with the vertical *arpeggi* illustrating '*Todesstille fürchterlich*' (a fearful deathly silence) and absolute immobility" (1978, 52).

"Wandrers Nachtlied I" (Wanderer's Night Song I), "Der du von dem Himmel bist," D. 224 (1815)

> *"You heavenly ones, I'm so tired of struggling! What's the point of all this pain and joy? Sweet peace, come, ah, come into my breast!"*

Schubert's setting of the young Goethe's prayer for inner tranquility is a through-composed song built from flexible lyrical writing that clings to the words like a proverbial glove. Schubert allows for one melodic effusion to serve as the song's climax, the repeated little "aria" on the words, "Sweet peace, come, ah, come into my breast!" (Süsser Friede! / Komm, ach komm in meine Brust!). This poem and the song it inspired together form a miniature that paradoxically encompasses a lifetime of experience.

"Heidenröslein" (Wild Rose), D. 257 (1815)

"A boy saw a wild rose growing in the meadow. I'm going to pluck you, wild rose! The rose said, I will prick you, so you'll remember me. And the rough boy plucked the rose; she pricked him, but it did no good."

Goethe's poem is based on an Alsatian folk song, which he refined into one of the most famous lyrics in European literature. The archetypal stories of seduction and abandonment, innocence and experience are distilled to their essence in less than two minutes of poetry and music. Schubert's strophic setting is the most perfect musical vessel imaginable for these words. Its "morgenschön" (beautiful as morning) purity is a test for each interpreter's powers of imagination, dramatic characterization, and above all, tact and artistic restraint.

"An den Mond" (To the Moon), D. 259 (1815) and D. 296 (1819?)

"Once again you fill the valley with your gleam. Laughter and kisses flow away. Happy is he who has one true friend."

Here is a poem set by the composer in two completely different ways, and each a masterpiece. The first version, D. 259 of August 1815, is a strophic setting that has been disparaged by most commentators on Schubert's songs, who prefer the more complex rendering found in D. 296. The fact that these critics are wrong has been proven by all the singers who continue to perform and record D. 259. Its noble, gorgeous, indelible melody is one of the most beautiful in German song and, as with all fine strophic songs, melody and accompaniment perfectly capture the quality of Goethe's words. It is one of Schubert's most lovable songs.

But D. 296, composed about four years later, is a great song too. This is a deeply sensitive modified strophic version of the poem. Decades before the impressionists, Schubert created a musical sound that suggests the silver moonlight inspiring the protagonist's ruminations. The different structure allows the composer opportunities for individuated expression of the poem's different sections that were impossible in the strophic D. 259. Fischer-Dieskau believes the composer has here excelled the poet at his own game: "Music such as this beggars all the description, all the imagery, all the characterization of the poem itself" (1978, 53). How wonderful that we have both versions, two such different responses to the same poem!

"Erlkönig" (The Erlking), D. 328 (1815) (CD Track 2)

A father on horseback clutching his sick child is galloping through the night in rough weather. The Erlking, an evil spirit, attempts to lure the child. The boy cries out but the father thinks his child is imagining it all. The Erlking pounces on the child, who dies in his father's arms before they reach home.

The poem is based both on Danish folklore involving an "elf king," mistranslated into German as the "alder king" (*Erkönig*), as well as personal experience. Goethe once underwent a terrifying night ride while carrying his young ward through wild weather on horseback (Whitton 1999, 204). Along with "Gretchen am Spinnrade," "Erlkönig" stands as the second pillar of the Goethe settings and of the entire genre of German lieder: another innovative masterpiece that reveals both the bewildering variety of the poet's vision and the teenage composer's uncanny ability to match him. The elemental power of the accompaniment has never lost its ability to startle listeners, conjuring images of the wild night, the rushing horse, and the primal terror of the father and son. The pianist plays incessant triplets requiring virtuosic execution while also bringing out the lurching, up-and-down motif in the bass (0:02), which captures the sensation of terror perhaps more effectively than any other passage in Western music.

The singer must have extraordinary histrionic talent to do justice to the quadruple roles of narrator (0:22), father (0:53), child (1:01), and demon (1:25) without distorting the contours of the composition. The Erlking's music is unnervingly sweet and seductive. He promises "games" (Spiele; 1:33) and professes his "love" (Ich liebe dich; 2:54) and physical attraction for the boy, which naturally increases the boy's terror (3:04). The boy's repeated cries to his father, "Mein Vater, mein Vater" (1:47, 2:26, 3:05), are almost unbearable in their shrill dissonance. This reaches its climax when the monstrous being seems to lunge directly at the boy on "If you won't come willingly, I'll force you" (Und bist du nicht willig, so brauch' ich Gewalt; 2:59). The low note on "Gewalt" (force) should be visceral; more frightening than all that has gone before (it is understated on the accompanying recording). As the boy loses consciousness, the horse "riding," marked "fast" at the outset, becomes "ever faster" (3:22) as the father struggles to reach home. The incessant pulse stops at the house door (3:39); the "narrator's" vocal line becomes a kind of half-spoken recitative: "In his arms the child [rest] was dead" (In seinen Armen das Kind war tot). The vocal rests that italicize "war tot" (3:44), the sudden silence of the piano, create a heart-stopping moment. The piano's gruff closing chords (3:50) end the song with a quick, brutal gesture.

It is an unsettling detail that the Erlking's menacing music always emerges out of the piano accompaniment following the comforting music characterizing the father. The song presents us with two fathers, one wholesome, one demonic—a kind of duality often encountered in Schubert's work. Whenever we are wracked by fear of the unknown, by a nameless existential threat, from the roar of thunder to the turbulence on an airplane, we recall the father's terrifying ride through a mysterious, infinitely hostile natural world. The grip of naked fear has never been better portrayed in any art form. One of the highest purposes of art is to remind us of our precarious place in the cosmos. Schubert's "Erlkönig" does this as well as any tragedy by Sophocles or Shakespeare.

"Harfenspieler Lieder": The Three Songs of the Harper, D. 478, 480, 479

Goethe's novel *Wilhelm Meister's Apprenticeship* offers two of the greatest characters in German literature, both indigent musicians: the mysterious, otherworldly waif Mignon, and her strange guardian, the Harper. The book contains several lyrics sung by these characters, representing their musical performances within the action of the novel. These lyrics are known to German speakers the way poems of Keats or Shakespeare are drilled into English-language students. A German friend once told me the only words her aged, dying father could recall were some of the Harper's forlorn lyrics, "Those who have never eaten their bread with tears"—childhood lessons meeting his present extremis, art's way of helping us both live and die. The Harper is an existential loner, tortured by guilt over his incestuous relationship with his sister, which produced his daughter/niece Mignon. Romantics were fascinated by incest. One thinks of Byron's real-life relationship with his sister as well as Siegmund and Sieglinde in Wagner's *Die Walküre*. Above all, the Harper symbolizes the outcast artist living on the edges of society, a figure with which Schubert strongly identified. Schubert was fascinated with the Harper's songs and made several attempts to set them over the years. The three discussed here, in the order Schubert wanted them sung, represent a kind of mini-song cycle, all in the key of A minor, which strongly anticipates the *Winterreise* cycle of 1827. Schubert's preoccupation with these Harper texts—note the dates for D. 480 alone—give the lie to the myth of Schubert as the unthinking clairvoyant rattling off song settings on a single breath of inspiration.

"Wer sich der Einsamkeit ergibt" (Whoever Chooses Solitude), D. 478 (1816)

> *"Whoever chooses solitude is soon alone; everyone leaves him to his anguish."*

The piano prelude captures the Harper's preparatory strumming. Marked "very slow," the song's gloom seems unrelenting until the key brightens and the piano becomes animated as he sings, "Yes, leave me to my sufferings!" (Ja! lasst mich meiner Qual!). The brief excursions to the major and the song's exquisite melismas suggest the Harper's masochistic streak. Only deeper pain and the grave can assuage his guilty anguish. The next section is unsettling on many levels. "Just as a lover sneaks up listening to tell if his mistress is alone, just so, day and night, suffering steals upon my solitude" (Es schleicht ein Liebender lauschend sacht, / Ob seine Freudin allein? / So überschleicht bei Tag und Nacht / Mich Einsamen die Pein). Goethe's words are wonderfully slithery, and Schubert's music matches him in musical gesture. Suffering is made unwholesomely erotic in verbal and musical imagery that recalls his incestuous transgressions with Mignon's mother. The postlude seems to sink downward as the Harper imagines his own death.

"Wer nie sein Brot mit Tränen ass" (Those Who Have Never Eaten Their Bread with Tears), D. 480 (1816/1822)

"Those who have never eaten their bread with tears, never cried in bed all night, will never know you, you heavenly powers."

The prelude, the Harper's eery figurations again, strikes a tone of desolation rare even in Schubert's most tragic music. Another "slow" tempo is requested, challenging pianist and singer to sustain the tension. The poem's two stanzas are each repeated to subtle melodic variation. Particularly memorable is the last reference to the "heavenly powers" (himmlischen Mächte), where the singer is given a wonderfully vulnerable high-lying melisma, capturing the song's opening pathos. The second stanza presents music of heroic defiance. The "heavenly powers" are now accused of cruelty as the Harper strums with a new sense of defiance that foreshadows the anger of *Winterreise*'s protagonist. "For all guilt is avenged on earth" (Denn alle Schuld rächt sich auf Erden) inspires the jarring, loud chords that occupy the closing measures, disorienting the listener. Are they the musical indication of punishment? Rather than rendering closure to the song, these chords make the last notes hang in the air like an unanswered question, which the third and final song may "answer." This is surely one of the strangest endings of any song.

"An die Türen will ich schleichen" (I Will Steal from Door to Door), D. 479 (1816)

> *"I will steal from door to door, silent, humble. People will think themselves lucky when they see me; they'll shed a tear, and I won't even know why."*

We are startled now by a steady, marching pulse, unlike the languishing tempi of the first two songs. The suicidal anguish has been sublimated into a strict formal structure. The keyboard writing seems modeled on Bachian counterpoint like that of the last prelude of the first book of *The Well-Tempered Clavier*, whose sad tread probably represents, given Bach's interest in religious symbolism, the steps of Christ on his way to Golgotha. The victim here is only too human, too sinful, and the transcendence that Schubert suggests for the incestuous Harper is one of the most boldly humanistic elements in all of the composer's music. The lines of both voice and piano are gently ever rising and falling. The most pathetic of images is delivered in music of the utmost intellectual and emotional restraint, rendering the song a masterpiece of tragic power.

"Mignon und der Harfer" (Mignon and the Harper), D. 877, no. 1 "Nur wer die Sehnsucht kennt" (Only the One Who Longs) (1826)

> *"Only the one who longs knows what I suffer."*

This lyric was later set by Tchaikowsky in a version that was once very popular in concert performance as "None but the lonely heart." Schubert made many attempts to set this poem. The last and greatest is this most remarkable of his vocal duets. It is set in B minor, Schubert's key signaling anguished longing or eroticism. This is music of such grounded primal suffering that one might be excused for misidentifying it as some kind of Jewish cantorial lament. The way the male and female voices interweave over the often frighteningly hollow piano accompaniment can leave a shattering impression. Especially effective is the section where both grieve for their nameless lost love who dwells "far away" (in der Weite), the harmonies beautifully suggesting vast, unbridgeable distances of longing. The vocal declamation achieves a real operatic largess as the father and daughter recoil in their agonies, "My head is swimming, I burn inside!" (Es schwindelt mir, es brennt / Mein Eingeweide). This is what a great Schubertian operatic duet would have sounded like had he been more fortunate in the genre.

"Ganymed" (Ganymede), D. 544 (1817)

"How you envelop me in morning radiance, Spring, my beloved! Where to? I go upward to your bosom, all-loving Father!"

Ganymede was a beautiful boy in Greek mythology with whom Zeus fell in love, spiriting him up to Mount Olympus to serve as the cup-bearer to the gods as well as his lover. In Shakespeare's *As You Like It*, Rosalind disguises herself as "Ganymede" when she dresses as a man and teases her lover, Orlando. In the romantic era, in addition to his obvious homoerotic significance, Ganymede also represented the desire of humankind to unite directly with the godhead in a spiritual as well as carnal sense. He symbolized the primal romantic longing to recapture the long-lost connection between mankind and the rest of creation in a condition of blinding wholeness. Goethe and Schubert seamlessly fuse all of these elements, the carnal and the spiritual, in this extraordinary work.

Marked "somewhat slow," the song has an ingratiating, ambling gait as the young man finds himself within his beloved natural world. "Ganymed" is above all a spring song, a love song to nature and the invisible forces that drive it. The erotic and the spiritual collide as the music finds a new urgency; Ganymed cries, "I come, I come! Where? Ah, where?" (Ich komm', ich komme! / Ach wohin, wohin?). The music builds to a melodic ecstasy as Ganymed senses he is being drawn up toward the heavens. "The clouds come down for me out of love" (Es schweben die Wolken / Abwärts, die Wolken / Neigen sich der sehnenden Liebe). The song closes with the boy's expression of adoration for the "All-loving father!" (Alliebender Vater!), sung to luxuriant melismas. Goethe famously described metaphysical experience as "the fall upward," and Schubert's music instinctively realizes this.

"Liebhaber in allen Gestalten" (A Lover in All Shapes), D. 558 (1817)

"I wish I were a fish so you'd angle for me. I wish I were gold, so I could serve you. But you'll have to take me as I am!"

If sunlight could sing, this is the music it would make. Here is a perfect fusion of text and tone. The singer's delightful banter somehow mixes innocence and seduction within the bouncy melody. The often scampering piano punctuates the strophic song's lyrics with its irresistibly witty theatrical asides. This is one of Schubert's most unforgettable songs, sparkling with a truly Mozartian humor and purity of utterance.

"Geheimes" (Secret), D. 719 (1821)

"Everybody is puzzled at my sweetheart's glances, but I know just what they mean. They are saying: I love this man, not any other."

This is Goethe and Schubert at their most flirtatious. The gentle, "somewhat fast and sweet" tempo with its "tiptoeing" accompaniment (in John Reed's phrase) creates the amorous atmosphere, the magic of a hidden flirtation and burgeoning love affair. The charming vocal line is uttered in discreet tidbits of text, frequently punctuated by rests. Perhaps someone who shouldn't be in on the "secret" is passing by? These rests help the singing actor to build the song's sense of reality.

This is text setting of a psychological insight encountered only once or twice in a century. It is used here to create a most heartwarming song. Reed aptly calls "Geheimes" "A kind of secret drama" (1985, 238).

"Suleika I," D. 720 (1821) (CD Track 3)

"What does this stirring mean? Is the east wind bringing me good news? Soon I'll find my beloved."

One of the greatest "Goethe" settings happens to be a poem not written by Goethe at all. Marianne von Willemer (1784–1860), one of Goethe's lovers, was the author of this poem, which Goethe included (along with her "Suleika II") in his *West-East Divan* collection; the literary borrowing was only revealed long after Goethe's and Schubert's deaths. Willemer's verses describe her longing for Goethe to arrive for a tryst at Heidelberg. Schubert made a delightful setting of "Suleika II" as well, but that work pales in comparison with this present composition. Brahms believed "Suleika I" to be the greatest of all German songs, and it's not difficult to see why. The song is a feast for the senses and emotions rare even for Schubert. The through-composed style allows maximum expressive variety while the craftsmanship ensures the work's perfect cohesion.

The opening gesture from the piano (0:00–0:15), as if the wind has lifted the leaves and dust into our atmosphere, is unlike anything else in Schubert. It is followed by a more familiar gestural companion of the composer (0:16), an insistent rhythmic pattern and the longing melody it enlivens. This is music close to that of the opening movement of the B Minor "Unfinished" Symphony from the following year. A similar melody and rhythm animates a contemporary song, "Der Zwerg" (discussed in Chapter 5). These are musical symbols of obsessive erotic longing. To this melody and rhythm, the lover asks her first anxious opening questions (0:19). Quickly the tonality and melody shift to the major (0:52) as she lovingly describes the "dust, insects, and leaves" that have been stirred to life (Kosend spielt er mit dem Staube, / Jagt ihn auf in leichten Wölkchen, / Treibt zur sichern Rebenlaube / Der Insekten frohes Völkchen). The song's constant shifting from B minor to major is miraculously seductive. The thought of her flushed cheeks (1:19) returns us to the minor; the wind's "gentle whisper" (leises Flüstern) brings us back to a passion-charged major (1:53). The upper regions of the piano color her happy expectation (2:12). "Over where the walls glow, I shall find my lover" (Dort wo hohe Mauren glühen, / Dort find ich bald den Vielgeliebten; 2:46–2:59). This music builds to an orgasmic climax, attaining a plateau from which the keyboard gently eases the protagonist back to earth (3:17). The last verse, which is repeated luxuriantly over and over, is a frank portrayal of postcoital repose (3:22–5:14). This is Schubert's most overtly erotic music.

"Der Musensohn" (The Son of the Muses), D. 764 (1822) (CD Track 4)

> *"I roam through field and forest, piping my song; all keeps time with me! Dear Muses, when shall I at last find rest on her breast again?"*

The poet envisions himself a "wingfooted" (Sohlen Flügel) musician breathing the inspiration of the divine muses, setting the entire world dancing and singing. This gift comes, however, at the cost of separation from home and love. Schubert's modified strophic setting is one of his most beloved songs. Its dancing, driving rhythm builds in expressive power through each repetition. Goethe's wonderful language is made even more glorious in this musical raiment. The bumptious accompaniment signals the song's good humor at the outset (0:00–0:06). A good singing actor will find subtle variety of emphasis from verse to verse, bringing out the ringing, heroic quality of the melody as well as finding room for the humorous characterization of the "stupid boy and the awkward girl" (Der stumpfe Bursche . . . Das steife Mädchen; 1:26–1:38). A good performance must also, without distorting the song's cheerful pulse, bring out the pathos of the last lines (1:40–2:01), the poignant image of the artist who unites his fellow creatures in joy yet is compelled to leave what he loves and wander "far from home" (weit von Haus).

"Wandrers Nachtlied II" (Wanderer's Night Song II) "Über allen Gipfeln ist Ruh" (Over All the Mountain Peaks There Is Peace), D. 768 (1822)

"Over all the mountain peaks there is peace. Wait, soon you'll find rest too."

Goethe wrote the poem, one of the briefest and most perfect of lyrics, while resting on a mountaintop. Closely akin to the earlier "Wanderer's Night Song," this poem and Schubert's setting achieve the seemingly impossible by exceeding even that song's concision and intensity of expression. The melodic lift given the word "soon" (balde) in the repeated phrase "soon you will find rest too" (balde / Ruhest du auch) is breathtaking. The extremely brief piano prelude and postlude create and sustain the mood while containing depths of feeling few composers have ever encompassed. Fischer-Dieskau observes, "There is nothing in music to equal Schubert's concentrated 14-bar epigram" (1978, 187).

* * * *

One year and five months after the death of Schubert, the eighty-year-old Goethe received a visit from the great singing actress Wilhelmine Schröder-Devrient. A witness reports: "Among other things, she sang him Schubert's setting of the 'Erlking,' and although he did not approve of poems [being through-composed], preferring the strophic style, the incomparable Wilhelmine's highly dramatic performance nevertheless moved him so deeply that he took her head between his hands and kissed her on the forehead, saying: 'Thank you a thousand times for that magnificent piece of artistry.' Then he added: 'I once heard that setting before and it did not appeal to me at all; but performed like this, the whole thing shapes itself into a visible image'" (E. Genast quoted in Goethe 1966, 218).

Other German Poets

Friedrich von Schiller

The ballads and lyrical poetry of Friedrich von Schiller (1759–1805) place him only slightly below his friend Goethe. Schiller's plays, however, including *Mary Stuart* and the *Wallenstein* trilogy, distinguish him as Germany's greatest playwright before Brecht. Both Beethoven and Verdi adored Schiller not only for his dramatic grandeur but also for his exceptional liberal humanism. The choral finale of Beethoven's Ninth Symphony is based on a Schiller lyric. Verdi created three operas based on Schiller's plays; one of these, *Don Carlos*, is arguably his greatest opera. Schubert set many Schiller lyrics, mostly during the early part of his career. These include several unwieldy ballads that can take as long as half an hour to perform. These ballads are some of the only music Schubert wrote that has not successfully braved the passing of the centuries. But the shorter Schiller lyric settings are another matter. Two are especially worth getting to know.

"Gruppe aus dem Tartarus" (A Gathering in Hell), D. 583 (1817) (CD Track 5)

> *"Listen! A cry like the anguished ocean! They are wracked with pain. 'Is the end near?' they ask. Eternity swings in circles above them, shattering Saturn's scythe."*

Schiller, in only a few lines, offers an image of hell recalling the epic visions of Dante and Milton. Schubert's setting matches and even transcends the poetic original. The twenty-year-old composer creates a flexible, arioso and recitative style for the singer that perfectly suits each passage of the poem. The keyboard writing is of a genuinely infernal power not encountered again until the masterworks of Liszt. Schubert is here setting poetry with a genius matched only by Monteverdi and Bach before him. The piano's opening, a rising crescendo (0:00–0:21), creates a avalanche of dissonance virtually unprecedented in Schubert's time. The rapid pulse of the piano and the dragging pace of the vocal writing create a vivid image of souls caught in a maelstrom. The dissonant, elongated setting of "weint" (weeping; 0:37) is the first "human" detail to reach our ears. Schiller's grating alliteration on "schweres, leeres" (heavy, empty) is eerily elongated (0:46–0:50) as the musical surge reaches its first climax. A new angry, limping tune (0:57) sets the next lines, "Schmerz verzerret / Ihr Gesicht, Verzweiflung sperret / Ihren Rachen fluchend auf" (Pain distorts them as they beg with mouths agape). These are the damned; their pride has led them to this pass. The image of their tears, however, makes their humanity irresistible to the composer, and an unexpectedly lovely arioso emerges (1:27) on "Folgen tränend seinem Trauerlauf" (they weep as they follow the sad course). Schubert here attains something of Dante's terrible pathos.

But their torments soon resume as the piano segues into dissonant, anxiously building chords (1:42). "They fearfully ask each other in whispers, 'Is the end coming?'" The question, "Ob noch nicht Vollendung sei?" is sung over and over, creating a tension almost without parallel in song literature, until the awful answer, "Ewigkeit" (Eternity) erupts in C major (2:11) to a blinding cascade of piano figuration. After reiteration of this powerful idea, the minor key and its dissonance return (2:49). The postlude suggests the souls are swallowed up, dragged into the anonymous darkness of the piano's lower register. An ironical arpeggio (3:02) serves as the song's "last word," like bubbles rising to the surface of a newly placid sea.

"Die Götter Griechenlands" (The Greek Gods), D. 677 (1819)

"Beautiful world, where are you? Your fields are deserted; no god is in sight."

German romantics were particularly interested in the heritage of classical Greece. In the early nineteenth century they embodied this longing for a lost antiquity in poetry, architecture, even clothing styles. This song of nostalgia for ancient Greece is, appropriately enough, built out of melodic fragments and broken arioso. It recalls a shattered column in an abandoned temple where bits of beauty survive amid the irreplaceable gaps caused by time. The first two measures for the keyboard are of extraordinary originality. The chords form a sad, unresolved refrain like "a wistful question" (Capell 1957, 158). The singer's insistent query, "Beautiful world, where are you?" (Schöne Welt, wo bist du?) haunts the song like a leitmotif. The main key of A minor is punctuated by several lovely little tunes in a wistful A major recalling the "fair springtime of nature" (Holdes Blütenalter der Natur) and Western civilization. But these A major fragments are no match for the pull back to the song's main key. A new sad tune in a halting rhythm proclaims that "no divinity appears before my eyes" (Keine Gottheit zeigt sich meinem Blick); "Only the shadow remains" (Blieb der Schatten nur zurück). The falling note pattern on "Schatten" is echoed on the piano and leads to a recapitulation of the opening, unanswerable question that resonates with all the unquenchable longing of romanticism. Schubert later recalled this song's opening in the Minuetto of his A Minor String Quartet, D. 804.

Matthias Claudius

Matthias Claudius (1740–1815) was an Enlightenment poet who edited his own literary journal. Schubert set more than a dozen of his poems during his early career, none as important as this one.

"Der Tod und das Mädchen" (Death and the Young Girl), D. 531 (1817) (CD Track 6)

> The Girl: *"Get away from me, you horrible skeleton! I'm still young, don't touch me!"*

Death: *"Give me your hand, you beautiful, tender thing! I'm a
          friend, not a punisher. Be of good cheer! I'm not rough,
          you'll sleep softly in my arms!"*

Nothing better exemplifies Liszt's description of Schubert's songs as "brief, mortal conflicts." This is a kind of duet for one singer-actor with a good low D. The death theme sounds in the solo piano (0:00–0:25), setting the scene of grim reckoning, reminding us of its omnipresence and inevitability. The theme's rhythm may have been inspired by the slow movement of Beethoven's Seventh Symphony, but Schubert has made it entirely his own, utilizing it in other works to suggest natural processes. After a short pause, the girl enters the scene in a hurried tempo (0:27), her words broken up by frequent rests depicting her panting terror. On the turn of a single rest, her vocal and physical pulse begin to slow (0:41) as she repeats "and don't touch me" (Und rühre mich nicht an) to a gentle, drooping figure. The following rests in the vocal line (0:47–0:53) signal more than her breathless silence as the piano segues back to the opening theme. Death's response (beginning at 0:54) is one of the most sublime moments in all music. His melodic material is almost entirely static, the musical embodiment of rest and consolation. In closing, however, his voice thrillingly plumbs its depths on his promise of peaceful sleep (schlafen; 1:45). The piano's postlude repeats the death motif over several bars, the sound of a merciful eternity. Schubert utilized the death theme for the variations movement in his D Minor "Death and the Maiden" String Quartet, D. 810, of 1824. One of his greatest songs thus inspired one of his greatest instrumental works.

Georg Philipp Schmidt

After luminaries like Goethe and Schiller, Georg Philipp Schmidt (1766–1849) is the most obscure figure imaginable: he's often referred to simply as "Schmidt from Lübeck." For all that, he managed to craft this poem, which embodies the idea of the romantic wanderer. Along with "Erlkönig," "Der Wanderer" was Schubert's most famous song in his lifetime. One of its melodies inspired the "Wanderer" Fantasy, his first mature masterpiece for solo piano. He would recall the song's introduction near the end of his life in a menacing passage from the development section of the B-flat Major Piano Sonata's opening movement (Badura-Skoda 2007, 122).

"Der Wanderer" (The Wanderer), D. 493 (1816) (CD Track 7)

> *"I came from the mountains. Where is my beloved land, where my language is spoken? A ghostly whisper answers, "There, where you are not, there is your happiness!"*

This song is like a romantic operatic scene, building vivid pictures of the protagonist and his environment. Marked "very slow," the opening is one of the most spine-tingling in Schubert's oeuvre. Doom-laden triplets gain in volume until they back off suddenly on the wanderer's first words (0:27), the musical equivalent of a suspenseful tracking shot in a movie scene. The wanderer's opening words foreshadow the first utterances of Wagner's Flying Dutchman some thirty years in the future; each character declaims his opening lines over an accompaniment depicting the forbidding natural world surrounding him. Also like the Dutchman, Schubert's wanderer stirs pity as well as unease and awe. His vocal line moves with unpredictable fluidity from declamatory recitative (0:27) to lyrical arioso (1:09). The famous wanderer theme is heard only once (1:44), setting the passage describing the coldness of the sun (Die Sonne dünkt mich hier so kalt) and his condition of being "a stranger everywhere" (ein Fremdling überall, 2:17). The wonderfully sad tune is only needed this once and is discarded for the rest of the song. This is the work of a disciplined musical dramatist. The song's tempo quickens (2:32), brimming with excitement as he pictures his homeland, where his friends are, where his language is spoken. But the excitement literally leads him to where he started, as the question "Where are you?" (Wo bist du?, 3:14) returns the music to its original slow, dolorous pulse. His earlier arioso returns (3:30), sounding all the sadder for the emotional journey that has ensued. In the final passage, the ghostly whisper that tells him he'll never be happy serves as the denouement. The wanderer finally comprehends his permanent, tragic estrangement as his voice descends sepulchrally (4:36) on the word "Glück" (happiness), which he now realizes he can never find.

Christian Friedrich Daniel Schubart

The musician and poet Christian Friedrich Daniel Schubart (1739–91) suffered greatly for his revolutionary political views. He was kicked out of university and later dismissed from a musical post for his egalitarian ideas, eventually enduring a ten-year prison sentence without trial for satirizing a German prince. But Schubert's most significant setting of his near namesake's work is the very unpolitical song below.

"Die Forelle" (The Trout), D. 550 (1817)

> *"In a clear stream the spirited trout darted like an arrow. I watched the happy little fish. Nearby a fisherman watched as well. The fisherman muddied the water, catching the trout, and my blood boiled."*

Schubert deleted the final verses that make the original poem a warning for young women not to be caught by "angling" young men. This cut was the first step toward creating a masterpiece. Schubert takes the first three verses of "Die Forelle" at their word and crafts a musical structure that reflects both the life cycle of the earth and the progress from innocence to experience. The song delivers both delight and emotional power through the folklike naivety of its melody. Its enormous popularity led to the creation of Schubert's happiest large-scale chamber work, the so-called "Trout" Quintet, D. 667, of 1819, named for the variation movement based on the already famous melody.

The bubbling accompaniment captures the exultant darting of the happy fish. The singer's incomparably radiant melody completes a musical depiction of nature at peace with itself. Not even the "cold-blooded" fisherman's appearance in the second verse can disturb this happy scene. But just as a cloud can instantly mask the sun, the piano figuration turns darker and the vocal line veers to the minor, the long, flowing phrases now broken by startled rests as the singer witnesses the trout's undoing. The original melody returns for the closing iterations of "And with boiling blood I saw the betrayed creature" (Und ich mit regem Blute / Sah die Betrogne an). The happy theme is ironic in this new context. The reference to blood encourages one to imagine the trout's blood pouring into the sun-brightened stream. The piano's darting fish motif continues, as a postmortem postlude, like a once-happy memory in the singer's consciousness. Life must go on. There are literally other fish in the stream, and besides, the fisherman, like the trout, or the singer too for that matter, has to eat. It is easy to imagine this song being appreciated by Mahler, whose depiction of man's relationship to nature it so strongly anticipates.

Friedrich von Schlegel

Along with his more famous elder brother August Wilhelm, Friedrich von Schlegel (1772–1829) was one of the leaders in the German romantic movement. An important poet and critic in his own right, the younger Schlegel moved to Vienna early in the century and became a prominent intellectual figure there. It is not known if Schubert ever met him, but at least some of the composer's friends did. Schlegel's early poems, of which Schubert set sixteen, revel in romantic nature worship. Like Wordsworth's contemporary poetry, which saw "God in the flower," Schlegel's poetic world is numinous. He is a pantheist who detects divinity in both animate and inanimate nature. These ideas held a strong appeal for Schubert and helped to shape his own worldview during the years 1818 to 1820, when he composed the majority of his Schlegel lieder. Most of the Schlegel settings are marked by an intense melodic directness and understated charm, but some are of real grandeur.

"Im Walde" (In the Forest) (sometimes called "Waldesnacht"), D. 708 (1820)

"The roar of wind, God's wings, deep in the cool forest night. Lightning flares, leaps up like the power of thought. We feel here the winds of creation itself."

This is staggering music requiring a singer and pianist who can distinguish its many colors and hold together its vast shape. Schlegel's verses approach expressionism in his barely contained ecstatic vision of the stormy forest night. The forge of creation must be made suddenly perceptible to the song's audience through the performers' discipline and passion. The piano writing paints the turbulent winds, the forces that bring both creation and destruction to earth. Capell observes, "the murmurs and thundering announce the forest and mountain music of *Die Walküre*" (1957, 167). The singer-protagonist is the ideal romantic who must share his vision with us. His first line mixes tense recitative declamation, "The roar of wind, God's wings" (Windes Rauschen, Gottes Flügel), with melting arioso, "deep in the cool forest night" (Tief in kühler Waldesnacht), instantly laying out the song's vast emotional and descriptive scope. The first verse links the terror and beauty of nature embodied in the winds with the swiftness of human thought. The texture deceptively lightens in the next section with the dancing, elfin piano writing and declamation about the "wonderful fiery light" (Herrlich ist der Flamme Leuchten) that turns on a dime to the frightening *sforzando* hammer blows with menacing rolls in the piano's bass on "Fire, often pregnant with death" (Blitze, schwanger oft von Tod). "Quickly the flame flickers and flares" (Rasch die Flamme zuckt und lodert) is sung to keyboard fourths spiraling upward till both voice and piano take a hair's-breath pause before God is invoked to powerful vocal declamation and thunderous chains of chords on "as though summoned to God" (Wie zu Gott hinaufgefodert).

Now embodying "the eternal murmuring of soft springs" (Ewig's Rauschen sanfter Quellen), the music is soft and lyrical. The references to "alluring sadness" (Trauer ... lockend) conjures a long-breathed melody full of Schubertian ambivalence between joy and sorrow. These "alluring waves" of sadness "bear our spirit far away" (Fernab hin der

Geist gezogen, / Die uns locken, durch die Wogen). This marks the attainment of romantic nirvana, and Schubert gives it a luxuriant melody that prefigures a similar theme in "Die Allmacht" of five years later. An extended piano interlude brings us closer to the song's opening fury without leaving the safety of the human sphere. A final burst of melodic pleasure infuses the penultimate couplet, "We feel creation's winds permeate our souls" (Schöpferischer Lüfte Wehen / Fühlt man durch die Seele gehen). The last verse's music returns us to the song's opening material, masterfully reimagined. "Windes rauschen, Gottes Flügel, / Tief in dunkler Waldesnacht" (The roar of wind, God's wings, deep in the dark forest night) is sung over the wind's semiquavers as the forest night itself, like some kind of dream, rushes away on a long diminuendo. Artur Schnabel must have had "Im Walde" in mind when he said, "Beethoven is a mountain range and Mozart a garden. And Schubert is a forest in sunlight and in shadow."

Ludwig Uhland

Ludwig Uhland (1787–1862) was a major romantic poet and medieval scholar whose egalitarianism, like that of so many of Schubert's poets and personal friends, set him at odds with the oppressive institutions that surrounded him.

"Frühlingsglaube" (Spring Faith), D. 686 (1820)

> *"The breezes and fragrances are everywhere. The world becomes more beautiful every day. Now everything, everything must change!"*

Surely the poet express a longing for not only natural renewal but also—though it could never be openly expressed—political renewal. This song is as much a prayer as "Ave Maria," hinting at Schubert's pantheistic sensibility. (Black's *Schubert and Belief* is a useful examination of the composer's spiritual nature.) Just as the human figures and emotions portrayed in his songs are of a Shakespearean breadth and variety, so too the depiction of nature posits a world burgeoning with natural forces too many to name. The noble, hymnlike theme presses forward throughout the song with a quiet, yet firm conviction. The music contains the motion of the life-giving breezes. The piano's chordal textures suggest the echoing of "the farthest, deepest valley" (das fernste, tiefste Tal). The promise that "All will change" (alles wenden) is repeatedly delivered with boldly luxuriant melismas. But after each of these assertions the pianist is directed to resume the *più piano* dynamic characteristic of most of the song. Schubert's convictions are deep enough not to require gratuitous fortissimo underlining. Schubert scholar John Reed writes of "Frühlingsglaube" that "as an expression of the renewal of human hope it is unsurpassed" (Reed 1985, 233).

August Graf von Platen

August Graf von Platen (1796–1835) was an important German poet whose unhappy homosexual love affairs are reflected in his disarmingly touching verses. After unsuccessful stints as an army officer and later a playwright, he spent the rest of his life in Italy. Brahms would later create several powerful songs from Platen's verses.

"Du liebst mich nicht" (You Don't Love Me), D. 756 (1822)

> *"My heart is broken, you don't love me. What good is the moon and sun to me? You don't love me!"*

Here words, voice, and piano form an indissoluble unity rare even in Schubert. The music puts us inside the protagonist's sensibility at the moment he faces rejection. This is the only reality we perceive in either background or foreground, without the distraction of a spinning wheel or galloping horse. The piano, taking the suggestion of the first line "My heart is broken" (Mein Herz ist zerissen) enunciates its main motif, an instrumental dirge recalling something of the "Death and the Maiden" theme, also in A minor. This dirge pervades the whole song like an idée fixe, the motto of the protagonist's impossible, obsessive love. Dissonance is used freely to color the words, making the pain they express all the more visceral. When the melody briefly sweetens as the closing lines are repeated, the tragedy of unrequited love is renewed again in the audience's collective imagination. The song's tempo is "moderate"; for all the inferno of suffering found in Schubert's universe, there is virtually no room for self-indulgence. The other Platen setting, "Die Liebe hat gelogen" (Love Has Lied), D. 751 (1822), is of a similar power.

Friederich Rückert

The poetry of Friederich Rückert (1788–1866) inspired generations of lieder composers, none more than Mahler, who created two great song cycles on Rückert texts (*Kindertotenlieder* and *Five Rückert Lieder*). Rückert was a prolific poet and an important scholar whose immersion in Oriental languages and poetry strongly influenced his own verse.

"Dass sie hier gewesen" (That She Has Been Here), D. 775 (1822?) (CD Track 8)

"The east wind's fragrance tells me that you were here."

If ever a song required repeated hearings to unlock its secrets, this is the one. Schubert uses music to express what had been virtually inexpressible before, the presence of absence. The music of this short song anticipates the impressionists as well as the expressionists in articulating the most ineffable emotional and sensory experiences. The song seems to drift without tonality as the poet savors the sensations of the wind. This tonal uncertainty "must have horrified [Schubert's] contemporaries" (Fischer-Dieskau 1978, 196). C major is only established when the lover identifies the traces of his beloved's erstwhile presence (Dass du hier gewesen). A brief dancelike phrase emerges on these words (0:34) and is savored by both voice and keyboard. This is all the more appealing for the tonal uncertainty that surrounds it. But such grounding is short-lived as the melody stops in midstream and silence ensues. Again the rootless chords hang in the air (0:54) as the poet weeps for her absence, the only consolation coming with the hope that these tears will somehow tell his lover "that I was here" (Dass ich hier gewesen). Again the short-lived C major dance of joy appears (1:28). Newfound confidence builds to a new but related lyrical phrase (1:48), "How can beauty or love be hidden?" (Schönheit oder Liebe, / Ob versteckt sie bliebe?). But the drifting, tonally ambiguous chords reappear (2:04) and "Düfte" (fragrance) and "Tränen" (tears) are sung to languishing melismas (2:09–2:26) over the piano's wavering chords before the dance phrase restores another tenuously held harmonic center (2:30). The drifting chords sound yet again (2:42) before the "Düfte...Tränen" sequence recurs (2:48) in foreshortened form, bringing the song to rest in its elusive home key, the dance motif having the last say in keyboard writing (3:02–3:23) that seems ready to float off again into unstable tonality at any moment.

"Du bist die Ruh" (You Are Rest), D. 776 (1823)

"You are rest and peace; you are longing and what fulfills it. The temple of my eyes is lightened by your radiance alone. O fill it altogether!"

This is one of Schubert's most beloved songs. Its perfection is seemingly effortless, like that of the C Major Prelude that opens Bach's *Well-Tempered Clavier*. The first notes of this song's prelude anticipate the singer's phrase "Du bist die Ruh," creating a hushed atmosphere instantly. This phrase depicts a sexual relationship of perfect happiness and fulfillment that, in seeming paradox, at least to some people, finds its perfect expression in a music of timeless mysticism. The song must seem artless at every moment of its delivery or the purity of its conception will be destroyed. This is easier said than done. The song is to be performed "slowly," much of it softly, and yet the singer has to build two crescendos ending in fearsome high Gs and As on the passage "Dies Augenzelt / Von deinem Glanz / Allein erhellt" (The temple of my eyes is lit with your radiance alone). These powerful climaxes are each followed by a bar of silence before the music resumes quietly. All this keeps the singer ruthlessly exposed. This "exposure" is part of the work's meaning. The love Rückert describes requires individuals to open themselves to others with selfless honesty; so too does the re-creation of this song.

Friedrich Leopold Graf zu Stolberg-Stolberg

Friedrich Leopold Graf zu Stolberg-Stolberg (1750–1819) was a friend of Goethe. He dedicated this poem to the memory of his late wife, Agnes. Some forty years later, Schubert set it the year his own illness began, bestowing an immortality on husband and wife that not even Stolberg could have imagined.

"Auf dem Wasser zu singen" (To Be Sung on the Water), D. 774 (1823) (CD Track 9)

> *"Amid the shimmering, mirroring waves the boat glides like a swan. So too glides the soul. Soon I will vanish on loftier, more radiant wings than this, and escape changing time."*

This may be Schubert's best-loved "water" song. There could be no better example of a strophic lied. John Reed observes, "The repeated last line, with its heart-easing shift to the major" (as at 1:03, 2:09, and 3:17) "brings a sensuous shock of delight, so that each verse increases our pleasure and sense of anticipation" (1985, 54). The surging A-flat minor "current" in the piano depicts the sensation and the glitter of the waves as the setting sun illuminates them, lovingly buoying the singer and his unforgettable bittersweet melody. Like a Shakespearean sonnet, this song captures the most ephemeral and beautiful of experiences and gives it the gift of eternity. The time-forgetting sensuality of the boat ride directly reflects the life of the soul on earth. The song aches with the primal longing to possess the beautiful forever.

Ernst Schulze

A popular poet in Schubert's day, Ernst Schulze (1789–1817) produced work that was highly autobiographical. He developed one-sided romantic fixations on several women whom he proceeded to pursue mercilessly. Clearly, he was a deeply disturbed individual with a tenuous grip on reality, a fact that hovers below the surface of his passionate verses. He nevertheless possessed a literary skill allowing others access to his inner world. Schulze's projection of alienation and desperation doubtless spoke strongly to Schubert during the two years leading up to his discovery of Müller's *Winterreise* cycle. Schultze died of tuberculosis at age twenty-eight.

"Auf der Brücke" (On the Bridge), D. 853 (1825)

> *"Gallop on, no stopping, my trusty horse, through night and rain!*
> *It's been three days since I've seen her; my joy and my sorrow.*
> *Longing will guide the way."*

A story once circulated that Dietrich Fischer-Dieskau went up on his lines while singing this energetic song. His pianist, Gerald Moore, immersed in the relentless piano part, whispered tersely, "I can't help you, I'm too busy galloping!" This anecdote captures something of the song's quality of gleeful danger. The song contains more drama and astute character drawing than many an opera. The manic rider spurs his horse furiously throughout this breathless work. The protagonist exults in the terrors of the forest journey, which by his own admission is toward a woman whose feelings for him are ambivalent at best. "Auf der Brücke" is an archetypal fusion of romantic extremes; the wild natural setting and furious motion of the goaded horse serve as physical manifestations of the protagonist's obsessive love and half-admitted fear of rejection. It is interesting to try to distinguish the pianistic turmoil that belongs to the horses' hooves from that created by the phantasms passing through the protagonist's mind. The rumbling trills that occur when the rider tells us of the "many [female] eyes" (Manch Auge) he imagines "smiling" (lacht) at him invitingly is chilling, and clearly belongs to the latter category. At times, the singer's declamation lunges thrillingly and dangerously upward, as if he longs to vault headlong through space in his manic impatience. Johnson observes, "With his almost infallible instinct for empathizing with the deeper resonances of poetry, Schubert understands that this '*gutes Ross*' [good horse] and its rider will forever journey in a fruitless quest for peace. In *Auf der Brücke* there is no sense [as in another night ride song, *Erlkönig*] of starting at one point, and arriving at another . . . the composer was not deceived by the bluster and bravado, and neither should we be" (1989–97, 18: 28).

"Im Frühling" (In Spring), D. 882 (1826)

> "*I'm sitting on this hill where once, at the start of spring, I was so happy with her. Everything here is just as it was except love's happiness is gone!*"

This is arguably the greatest of Schubert's "spring" songs. The principal theme begun in the piano prelude is one of Schubert's most ingratiating and unforgettable. The sweet melody's sauntering rhythm is the very embodiment of the lazy, sunny day that sets the action of the poem. The vocal part begins with a variant melody (let's call it the B theme), which allows for wonderful mimetic effects. The rising and falling vocal line on "Das Lüftchen spielt im grünen Tal" (The breeze plays in the green valley) is particularly vivid. By the second verse, the voice is sharing in the heavenly spring tune with the piano. The lost love now enters the song, united with the protagonist in the stream's reflection. Between verses, the piano indulges us with the spring song again in delicious syncopation; all could not be more right in the world. The next two verses expand on this image of lost paradise. New music and the minor key make their inevitable intrusion, but the "new" music is just a minor key variant of the B tune—everything contains its opposite in Schubert. This is how he structures music as well as how he perceives the structure of experience. This new, anxious variant heralds the protagonist's realization of mutability and his tragic inability to abandon a love that is over. In Schulze's obsessive view—and what human has not shared this same sentiment at some point—"Love alone remains, and ah! Pain!" (nur die Liebe bleibt zurück, / Die Lieb', und ach, das Leid!). The piano segues back to the major as only Schubert knows how to do, breaking our hearts not in the minor, but in the major key. The spring theme supports the singer's fanciful longing to be a bird and sing of "her" the whole summer long. Is there a greater and more direct illustration in all music of Dante's maxim that "nothing is more painful than happiness recalled in misery"?

Johann Friedrich Rochlitz

The poet Johann Friedrich Rochlitz (1769–1842) was a critic and the founder of an important musical journal in Leipzig. He was also a friendly acquaintance and admirer of the composer.

"An die Laute," D. 905 (1827)

> *"Lightly sound, little lute, whisper to my love, but not so loud the jealous neighbor's sons hear you!"*

Here is an understandably popular and witty song. Rochlitz's enterprising, humorous wooer plays on forever, thanks to Schubert's delightful tune and the charming "lute strumming" of the piano's accompaniment. Both singer and pianist need to keep in mind the dramatic situation, that the whole serenade must be carried on clandestinely; after all, there's more than one jealous neighbor's son to contend with.

Karl Lappe

Karl Lappe (1773–1843) was a schoolmaster who later turned to farming. This highly obscure figure lives beside the starriest names in German literature because of two very different poems that are at the core of German art song.

"Der Einsame" (The Recluse), D. 800 (1825) (CD Track 10)

> *"When crickets chirp by my warm fire, I sit cozily by, happy and at peace. Chirp away, cricket in my little room; I enjoy the company."*

This song sums up much of what we imagine when we think of *gemüt-lichkeit*, that state of coziness and warm satisfaction that was so prized by the Austrian middle class in the turbulent early decades of the nineteenth century. This is a song rich in gentle humor. The vocal melody embodies contented self-satisfaction. The chortling piano part is one of Schubert's most lovable, capturing a man happily set in his ways and his snug little world. At one point (0:52) the grumbling in the bass gives sound to the ashes breaking under the poker. The man's voice is only momentarily agitated (2:30) when he briefly recalls "the bustle of the loud world that brings no contentment" (Was in dem Schwarm der lauten Welt . . . Gibt nicht Zufriedenheit). The song's last verse leaves him in his contentment, along with his sole companion, the cricket merrily chirping in the piano (3:20 and 3:40).

"Im Abendrot" (In Sunset Glow), D. 799 (1825) (CD Track 11)

> *"How beautiful your world is, Father, when the golden light streams through my little window! How could I ever complain or find trouble between you and me? Your heaven is in my heart, which will drink in the fire and savor the light until it breaks."*

This is the composer at his best, his most human, and his most mysterious. The tempo, "slow, solemn," is extreme for Schubert, but it allows time to stand still for a couple of precious minutes. This effect is helped by Schubert's relatively rare demand for the use of the sustaining pedal. The slow, gently rolling chords (0:00–0:23) herald a vocal hymn of gratitude to God for the beauty of his world at sunset. A foreshortened version of the opening prelude (1:48) introduces a modified second verse that begins with a climbing vocal line (2:02) asking, "Could I complain? Could I be afraid?" (Könnt' ich klagen, könnt' ich zagen?). But the upwardly moving voice with its harmonic and existential tension is immediately resolved in the next line with its steplike up-and-down motif (2:12) on "How could there ever be trouble between you and me" (Irre sein an dir und mir?), briefly redolent of some ancient church music in our collective consciousness. "No" (Nein), the singer confidently exclaims to a ringing E, which signals the song's climax (2:26). Spiritual contemplation leads the protagonist to divine that there is no distinction after all between inner and outer worlds. "I already bear your heaven in my heart" (ich will im Busen tragen / Deinen Himmel schon allhier). This inner peace, a religious revelation as convincingly portrayed as any in music, will sustain the protagonist till his last breath, a sentiment expressed in music of heartbreaking beauty. The piano's coda (3:26) allows this musical image of beatitude to fade into silence like the sun descending below the horizon.

Johnson writes: "The song passes as imperceptibly as the sunset it describes, and like a sunset it changes at the same time as seeming to stand still (the movement of the inner voices of the chords is masterful). This somehow discourages our curiosity to analyze what is happening; the music, like the moment of evening radiance, seems stationary and unending in its beauty. And then, just as suddenly, it is gone. This seems a metaphor for life itself which we imagine will last for ever but which is as precious as those few moments when the sun hangs in the sky before slipping gently over the horizon" (1989–97, 31: 42). When one considers all the sorrows and frustrations of Schubert's life, the idea that these verses would appeal to him, let alone inspire him to to create such a song, is comforting. If "Im Abendrot" were all he had left us, he would still be regarded as one of the world's greatest composers.

Schubert's Friends and Other Austrian Poets

chubert was an intensely social being whose friends not only materially sustained him as he eked out his existence as a composer but also often supplied him with their own poetic texts for songs. Most of Schubert's friends were dilettantes, but at least one, Mayrhofer, was a poet of genuine talent. If the verse "had music in it," Schubert could make lieder out of it. Contemporary Austrian poets supplied numerous lyrics that are among his most beloved and dramatically effective songs.

The first poet to inspire Schubert to songwriting was an Austrian woman. Gabriele von Baumberg (1775–1839) was called the "Sappho of Vienna." She became an accomplished poet and intellectual in a world where women were not taken seriously in such matters. She married a Hungarian radical whose Napoleonic enthusiasm led to the couple's banishment to Linz. Schubert's very first attempt at song composition in 1809 or 1810 appears to be "Lebenstraum" (Dream of Life), D. 39, a fragment of a setting of one of Baumberg's poems. Schubert scholar Susan Youens explores the reasons this woman's work so captivated the teenage composer. In the poem, Baumberg asserts "that artists should follow the vocation they know to be theirs, that the true artist should listen to her heart, not the advice of well-meaning friends or an ill-disposed society, no matter what price the world exacts in scorn and disapproval. Schubert, disputing with his father about the future course of his life, could have found in [Baumberg's] poetic dream additional justification for his belief in himself as a composer, all the more so because the obstacles faced by women were even more extreme than those of men" (1996, 27). From the beginning of his songwriting career Schubert had a strong empathy for women and female subjects, a trait shared with Mozart and Richard Strauss, who created exceptional female operatic characters. Schubert retained an interest in Baumberg's poetry for several years, creating at least one minor masterpiece, "An die Sonne" (To the Sun), D. 270 (1815?), which deserves to be better known. The "sinking sun" is apostrophized with music that delightfully, though accidentally prefigures the "Arietta" tune of Beethoven's final piano sonata some years later.

Franz von Schober

Schubert's best friend was probably Franz von Schober (1796–1882). A dashing Swedish nobleman and artistic dilettante, he inspired much jealousy among some of Schubert's more bourgeois friends. (See Chapter 3 for more details on this relationship.) Schubert's last letter is addressed to Schober, requesting him to drop off James Fenimore Cooper novels to keep the composer occupied in his sickbed. In later years, Schober became a friend of Franz Liszt, who found him a "noble spirit" (Clive 1997, 190). Perhaps history owes Schober something of a break in view of Schubert's own devotion to him.

"An die Musik" (To Music), D. 547 (1817)

> *"You holy art, how many times when life weighs me down, you have warmed me and shown me a better world. You sweet art, I thank you for this!"*

Here is another candidate for the title of Schubert's most famous song. It is a hymn to the art form to which he devoted his life and soul. Its even-flowing pulse anticipates another perfect love song from nearly a decade later, the Shakespeare setting "An Silvia." Virtually all lieder singers have "An die Musik" in their repertoire. The great German soprano Lotte Lehmann, who devoted much of her career to lieder, sang this as her final encore at her farewell recital. Not even her iron discipline could restrain her emotions as she came to the last line, "Du holde Kunst, ich danke dir dafür!" (You sweet art, I thank you for this!).

Johann Baptist Mayrhofer

Schubert set more poems by his friend Johann Baptist Mayrhofer (1787–1836) than by any other poet save Goethe and Schiller. (See Chapter 3 on Mayrhofer; Steblin [2001] has unearthed fascinating new information on this elusive, depressive man's life, including the identities of women he pursued romantically.) Mayrhofer's eventual suicide is tragically foreshadowed in much of his poetry.

"Nachtstück" (Night Piece), D. 672 (1819)

> *"When the night falls the old man picks up his harp and sings in the forest, 'O holy night! Soon, soon I'll sleep, forever free from trouble. Then the trees will rustle, "Sleep well, old man."' The old man listens and is quiet—death has called him."*

The poet's longing for death and transcendence is readily apparent. Perhaps Schubert felt he could imaginatively meet his friend halfway, envisioning himself as the aged bard, who after a long life, sings a lovely swan song and is mystically drawn into nature. Schubert creates a successful ballad out of Mayrhofer's strangely personal romantic vision. The piano's slow, often dissonant introduction serves as a mysterious C minor "overture" to the narrator's first arioso as he sets the scene of the dark forest. The slow-moving passage describing the old man's taking of his harp moves darkly within the piano's bass, creating an uncanny sense of expectation. Then comes the old musician's song, a rich aria of supplication. When nature finally responds, the song quickens and modulates movingly into C major. The song closes as we learn of the old man's death with fragments of the consoling broad, hymnlike tune being shared by the singer and piano. It is fascinating to compare this young man's fantasy of old age and idealized death to "Der Winterabend," Schubert's last meditation on old age, discussed below.

"Auflösung" (Dissolution), D. 807 (1824) (CD Track 12)

"Hide yourself, sun, I'm on fire with rapture! Sweet powers well up and encompass me with their singing. Dissolve, world, never disturb these sweet choirs!"

Besides the song's utter originality in sound and style, what shocks the listener is the positive, rhapsodic music Schubert has created for his friend's barely concealed vision of self-destruction. This song was composed during a period of his disease's recurrence, when the composer expressed a desire to be transmuted to a higher level of existence than that afforded his poor, suffering body. But for all that longing, Schubert, unlike Mayrhofer, never lost the will to live. Nevertheless, his unparalleled human understanding puts the composer inside the poet's morbid, neurotic personality, and this act of empathy and old affection creates a work that is true to the poet's intentions, yet at the same time paradoxically life-affirming—one of the supreme examples of German romanticism. The images of ecstatic dissolution, of immersion in divine, transfiguring fire conjured music from Schubert whose only parallel may be the otherworldly, ecstatic figurations that "purge" the theme during the variations at the end of Beethoven's Piano Sonata, Op. 109. Wagner's later manifestations of paradoxically healing destruction in *Tristan* and *Götterdämmerung* seem barely a step or two away.

The piano writing is orchestral in its density. The prelude contains "a rhythmic cell made up of a rising arpeggio to which is added a tiny shudder of ecstasy (0:00–0:11), a motif that is repeated nearly fifty times in the song" (Johnson 1989–97, 11: 22–23). The singer's rhapsodic melody soars loftily above the piano's intimations of immortality. A new ecstatic melody (1:01–1:11) raises the expressive tension even higher on "I am enveloped in heavenly singing" (Die mich umschlingen, / Himmlisch singen). As the singer dismisses all corporal reality on the emphatic repetitions of "Dissolve, World" (Geh' unter, Welt), the keyboard creates an almost visual gesture of vehement rejection in iterative, stabbing notes in the bass (1:12–1:19 and 1:31–1:38). The coda is built out of fervid, almost speechlike repetitions of "Dissolve, World" (2:05–2:13), a final moment of visceral shock. In this song of dissolving barriers, the division between song and speech shatters and the singer's world seems to enter that of the audience.

"Lied eines Schiffers an die Dioskuren" (Song of the Boatman to the Dioskuri), D. 360 (1822?) (CD Track 13)

> *"Dioscuri, twin stars, you light the way for my boat; your mild vigilance is a consolation on the sea. This oar that I ply shall hang as an offering at your temple when I get ashore."*

This poem is a prime example of Mayrhofer's classicism. Schubert created from it one of his noblest works. Another great nocturnal hymn graces this perfectly wrought ABA structure. The calm sea resides in the piano's gentle wave motion (0:00–0:53), held in quiescence by the twin divinities as the singer begins his hymn. The sea's menacing power makes itself felt only fleetingly in the double *forte* writing for voice and piano in the B section (0:53–1:07). This resistance of the sailor to the storm instantly mellows (1:11) as he concedes the added strength these gods provide him. The idea of man's heroic struggle with nature and his mysterious relationship with divinity is deeply Greek, and Schubert's setting reveals a sensitivity to the world of gods and heroes that Mayrhofer's friendship had opened to him. The last verse returns to the opening hymn (1:27), now animated by smooth-flowing fourths as the ship begins its glide toward land and the temple. Spaun recounted that when the singer Vogl, himself an ardent Hellenist, "saw Mayrhofer's *Dioskuren*, he said that it was almost incomprehensible that such profundity and maturity could come out of that tiny young man" (Fischer-Dieskau 1978, 95).

Matthäus von Collin

Poet and playwright Matthäus von Collin (1779–1824) was tutor to one of Napoleon's illegitimate sons. He was a cousin of Schubert's close friend Joseph von Spaun, who introduced him to the composer.

"Wehmut" (Melancholy), D. 772 (1822)

> *"When I walk through forest and field I feel both sad and happy.*
> *For everything that sounds and grows, man himself and all this*
> *beauty, shall vanish and go away."*

This two-page song is one of the most perfect of Schubert's compositions. The music breaks into two contrasting stanzas. The first is a nobly sad arioso where the words "Schönheit Fülle schau'" ([I] see the meadow in all its beauty) stand out through the gorgeous arabesque in the vocal line. The second section introduces the "sound" of time and change through the piano's eerie tremolos, which seem to invade the song much as the dreadful rumblings disturb the middle section of Chopin's "Raindrop" prelude. The little storm breaks to usher in an extraordinary coda. The singer repeats "und vergeht" (and goes away) over and over to the accompaniment of soft chords as the idea of universal loss weighs on him. The effect is the musical equivalent of Shakespeare's Lear facing the ultimate truth in his famous line, "Never, never, never, never, never."

"Der Zwerg" (The Dwarf), D. 771 (1822)

> *"In the gloomy light a boat floats by with the queen and her dwarf.*
> *He says, 'You forsook me for the king; only your death can gladden*
> *me. I'll hate myself forever, but you must die.' She prays, 'May*
> *you not suffer because of me.' The dwarf kisses her, then lowers the*
> *dying woman into the sea. He'll never come to shore again."*

The poem attests to the romantic fascination with the grotesque and outré sexuality. Like "Erlkönig," "Der Zwerg" is a horror ballad requiring exceptional acting talent from the singer. Schubert's music invests the words with reality through the dramatic declarations he creates for his narrator and the two characters as well as the exceptionally impassioned atmosphere. The singer-actor must make the outlandish situation credible in performance. Much of the song's depth resides in Schubert's refusal to portray the dwarf as a stereotypically evil character. Jane K. Brown observes, "He is not evil after all, but a sufferer at the hands of a heedless nature that created him a dwarf and not a king. . . . Like his Biedermeier contemporaries, Schubert had immense awareness of *Weltschmerz*, the generalized suffering of living in an apparently indifferent world." (1997, 190). The main theme with its obsessive one-two-three-*four* rhythm is very similar to that of the contemporary first movement of the "Unfinished Symphony." This is music expressive of impassioned longing. At twenty-five, Schubert was on the cusp of wider fame and a staggering mastery. It may also understandably have been the most sexually charged time of his life; sometime close to the creation of this song, he became infected with syphilis. "Der Zwerg" asserts that the composer already knew that the wages of passion can often be death.

"Nacht und Träume" (Night and Dreams), D. 827 (1822?)

> *"Holy night, and dreams float down, like moonlight through space into the silent breasts of men. When day awakens them, they cry, 'Come back, holy night! Sweet dreams, come back!'"*

The Enlightenment cherished reason and the bright light of day. One thinks of Mozart's triumph of light over darkness in *The Magic Flute* or Haydn's electrifying proclamation of "light" in the opening of *The Creation*. But the romantics rediscovered the dream and the beauty of darkness. Here they were anticipated by their great forerunner Shakespeare. Caliban in *The Tempest* extols the magic of dreams on his enchanted island, which would "show riches / Ready to drop upon me, that when I wak'd / I cried to dream again." One cannot imagine a better musical analogue to Caliban's lines than this lied. The gorgeous nocturnal song hovers over the gently pulsing keyboard that floods the soundscape. A tone of rapt, uncanny intimacy must be sustained by both performers throughout.

Johann Ladislaus Pyrker von Oberwart

Hungarian poet Johann Ladislaus Pyrker von Oberwart (1772–1847) was a priest who became the Patriarch of Venice. He was an admirer of the composer and met him first in Vienna and then by chance when both men were vacationing at Bad Gastein in the happy summer of 1825. Undoubtedly Schubert saw Pyrker as a good contact, but there is evidence that he truly respected him and felt some spiritual affinity with the older man's vision of the godhead.

"Die Allmacht" (The Almighty), D. 852 (1825)

> *"Great is Jehovah, the Lord! Heaven and earth proclaim his might.*
> *You see it in the waving corn, the flowers, the stars!"*

"The most sublime of Schubert's songs" is John Reed's judgment of "Die Allmacht," and he could well be right (1985, 149). This is also the most Wagnerian of all Schubert songs, requiring (preferably) a dramatic soprano with stage presence and vast reserves of vocal power and energy. No wonder it has been an important repertoire piece for singers such as Kirsten Flagstad and Jessye Norman. This song affords a view of Schubert the Titan, a composer who, when the occasion called for it, could create seemingly earth-shattering sound, projecting a cosmic musical perspective in service to a specific poetic image. The first C major bars of piano introduction set the scene with their mysterious, powerful chordal patterns, emerging from *piano*, cresting on a double *forte*, and then receding back to *piano*. A stage of immense size and depth, a scene expressive of power and tenderness are instantly set before our senses. The voice enters with its splendidly declamatory lines repeated over the thundering supporting chords—grand proclamations worthy of the enormity of the subject. The powers of the voice and the piano's hammers and strings are tested to their limits to express the unlimited. The harmonic progressions are truly awesome, but the Almighty is also present in the "gold waving corn" and "flowers," which inspire music of contrasting lyricism that must be sung by a voice that can just as easily handle tender melodic writing. The song ends in a titanic peroration built out of the opening material (in this respect recalling the awe-inspiring return of the chorale andante theme in the final bars of the contemporary Great C Major Symphony's first movement.) Cappel notes that this song is not designed "for general devotions" but is rather a work both "intensely personal and rapturous" (1957, 213).

Franz Xaver von Schlechta

The poet Franz Xaver von Schlechta (1796–1875) was a lifelong friend of the composer.

"Fischerweise" (Fisherman's Tune), D. 881 (1826)

"The fisherman has no cares. He sings while he works and working makes him happy. On the bridge over there the shepherdess is angling for a fish—sly minx, you're not catching this fish!"

"Fischerweise" contains much of what makes Schubert's songs so incomparable. The fusion of vocal and keyboard writing creating perfect chamber music, the effect of an intimate dramatic scene performed in a living room, vocal and instrumental writing at their most captivating, held together by Schubert's heartiest open-air music. This is a workman's song. He is a happy man at one with nature in ways the intellectual romantics can only dream about. The keyboard vividly creates the water and its happy motion. An honest day's work in the sun and on the waves becomes an image of God's grace. And if the "fishing" girl finally reels in the fisherman, so much the better for them both.

Friederich Reil

Friederich Reil (1773–1843) was an actor who played major roles at Vienna's Burgtheater.

"Das Lied im Grünen" (The Song of the Green World), D. 917 (1827)

"Into the green world! Spring invites us with his staff of flowers to where the birds and fields are! Let us follow the happy youth and when life is no longer green, we won't have missed the green years."

This nature song was written while the composer enjoyed a brief stay in the Vienna woods. It is a modified strophic song that in a good performance, one never wishes to end. Like the Rondo that closes the A Major Sonata, D. 959, Schubert creates music of self-renewing fecundity and health with a twinge of melancholy never far from the surface. The joyous flickering of dappled green and sunlight is reflected in the keyboard writing. One of the most remarkable moments is in the last verse when the poet concedes, "When life is one day no longer green" (Grünt einst uns das Leben nicht fürder), which on its repetition veers to the minor key while the words are declaimed to a single note. The premonition of death almost halts this long song in its final verse, but within an instant, Youens observes, Schubert "bring[s] back the songs of the larks, . . . he insists yet again on the wisdom, the shelter from terror, that is ours if we live to the fullest in life's green season. . . . What he makes of the dark specter haunting the Arcadian meadow makes of this lied one of the most quietly heroic compositions he ever wrote" (2002, 323, 322).

Karl Gottfried von Leitner

The Graz-based poet Karl Gottfried von Leitner (1800–90) was regarded as the most important Styrian poet of the time. Poet and composer never met. In old age, Leitner wrote to Schubert's nephew regarding his uncle's settings, "I believe that their excellence is vouched for by the fact that, whenever I hear them performed, I experience exactly the same emotions as I did when writing the words of the text" (Clive 1997, 116).

"Der Kreuzzug" (The Crusade), D. 932 (1827)

> *A monk stands in his cell and watches as the knights in armor ride through the meadow. They sing songs and depart on a ship. "I am a pilgrim too, though I stay at home. Life with its dangerous waves and burning sands is its own crusade into the promised land."*

This is a poem of lonely individualism, a Biedermeier equivalent to Milton's "Sonnet on his Blindness." This monk too serves who can "only stand and wait." In Milton's autobiographical lines and Leitner's fanciful setting, both men are sustained by their religious faith. The monk, like Lappe's cozy Einsamer and perhaps Schubert himself, possesses a hard-won contentment (Youens 2002, 236). The piano provides a firm harmonic bedrock for his hymn throughout the song until the stanza signaling his quiet realization, "The monk still stands at the bars" (Der Münich steht am Fenster noch), in which piano and voice change places, the piano taking the vocal line and the singer-protagonist intoning the harmonic basis of his existence. It is as if, Fischer-Dieskau observes, "the watcher were trying to join in the crusader's song" (1978, 274). This is such a simple device, yet it never fails to move an audience in a good performance.

"Des Fischers Liebesglück" (The Fisherman's Luck in Love), D. 933 (1827)

> *"The light from my beloved's window reflects onto the water. She steals down to join me in my boat. We kiss, we weep, we smile, we're halfway to heaven."*

Why is this music so haunting, so strangely anguished? If it is created from "emotion recollected in tranquility" (Wordsworth's definition of the origin of poetry), it is based on the memory of sexual passion recalled from beyond the grave, a new, uncanny phrasing of the dangerous passions that make up "Der Zwerg." The waves lap quietly as the lovers seek ecstasy in a place outside of light and time. This work is a kind of barcarolle, that is, a work in imitation of the songs of Venetian gondoliers. Chopin utilized this form for his world-embracing late work the *Barcarolle*, Op. 60. But this barcarolle is a very ghostly one. Schubert remarked in 1824: "People imagine that they can reach one another, but in reality they only pass one another by. Oh misery for him who realizes this!" (Schubert 1970, 76).

"Der Winterabend" (The Winter Evening), D. 938 (1828)

*"It's so still and comfy around me; the sun is set, the day is done.
The snow helps make things nice and quiet on the street outside.
I like to sit by the window and think far back, about her, and the
happiness of love, and sigh, and think."*

Schubert knew he would never live to old age, so he created an old
age for himself in this loving song of an ideal end to life, cast in his
most autumnal B-flat major. Like several of his other curmudgeonly
"Einsamer" protagonists, the old man of "Der Winterabend" has recon-
ciled himself to loneliness through his sense of the powers present in the
nonsentient world surrounding him. The moonlight is his companion,
as he thinks back, "so far, ah, so far" (ach weit, gar weit) to the time
of love's happiness. The piano writing is some of the most pictorially
and psychologically evocative in Schubert. The keyboard creates a
diaphanous cocoon for the old man reflecting the snow's soundproof-
ing, the fine-spun moonlight, and his own restful heartbeat. For all the
pleasures of silence and solitude, it is the memory of love that figures
most importantly for the old man and is treated to great elaboration
in the song's coda. "I think about her, and the happiness of love, sigh
silently and think, and think" (Denk' an sie, an das Glück der Minne,
/ Seufze still, und sinne, und sinne). Words and musical phrases repeat
in a sleepy mantra as the old man drifts away, the iterated Ds in the
piano's right hand gently suggesting the "passing bell" that marked life's
end in Biedermeier Austria.

Johann Gabriel Seidl

A friend of Schubert, Johann Gabriel Seidl (1804–75) was a popular
poet representing "the perfect incarnation of the *Biedermeier* style"
(S. Lechner, qtd. in Clive 1997, 212). He holds the accidental honor
of being the last poet whose work the composer would set ("Die
Taubenpost" in *Schwanengesang*).

"Der Wanderer an den Mond" (The Wanderer Addressing the Moon), D. 870 (1826)

"I'm on the earth, you're up in heaven, but we both keep moving.
I'm a stranger everywhere. The endless heaven is your homeland.
Happy the one who wherever he goes stands on his native soil!"

Though a (nondogmatic) Catholic, Schubert could distill the essence of a Protestant hymn in the opening Andante of the Great C Major Symphony. In this song, the jaunty minor key recalls the nature of Jewish folk song with its particular plangency, perfect for Seidl's wanderer, who is "homeless" (heimatlos) everywhere. The tempo is "rather fast." This wanderer keeps his tread firm in a hostile universe while strumming his guitar, represented by the piano's interludes. The moon's "happier" situation, wherever she strays is her homeland (Der Himmel, endlos ausgespannt, / Ist dein geliebtes Heimatland), inspires a transition to a wonderful major-key tune that then closes the song with a keyboard postlude resembling a lullaby. Fischer-Dieskau's analysis of this song's transition from minor to major is striking in its ramifications.

> The major-minor polarity . . . is the source of all musical tension: the contrast of masculine and feminine, of hardness and soft-ness, of light and shade, of day and night. Schubert was the first composer to breathe musical life into this elementary dramatic principle. It symbolized heaven and earth to him . . . and he united them. It is in the transition of one to the other that the essence of Schubert's art lies. During these hardly perceptible moments a metamorphosis occurs, a gliding-over into another realm. (197–198)

The unbridgeable gap between human instability and divine immu-tability is distilled in a matter of a few bars. The nature of existence is described here, and Schubert, through his music, reconciles us to it.

Other European Poets

Schubert's reading was wide and eclectic. His lieder contain a broad range of European poetry, including the Italian-language songs he set in his student days for Salieri, as well as Swiss poetry, German translations from Aeschylus, and Shakespeare and other British poets.

Anacreon

The oldest European poetry set by Schubert is a poem from the sixth century B.C. Greek Anacreon, in a translation made by a friend of the composer, Franz von Bruchmann (1798–1867).

"An die Leier" (To the Lyre), D. 737 (1822–23?)

> *"I want to sing heroic songs about the great Greek heroes, but my strings only sound music of love!"*

This splendid song, with its variety of heroic, witty, and tender elements, makes an excellent opening song for a recital. The singer, like some reincarnated rhapsode from antiquity, readies himself to sing of stern heroism. The keyboard's proud opening suggests the lyre, the harplike instrument to which poets such as Anacreon and Homer sang and chanted their poetry. All seems ready for a formal classical pastiche not unlike Gluck's Greek-themed operas, until the force of tender feeling disintegrates the piano-lyre's "heroic" strumming and the singer indulges in the generous arioso writing that heroic decorum simply cannot keep down. The singer complains, "But my strings only sound music of love" (Doch meine Saiten tönen / Nur Liebe im Erklingen). There is gentle humor in this song as the man wrestles with his performative obligation and his natural expressive impulses. There is pathos too, in the final passage set to new lyrical music, in which the singer "bids farewell" to the "heroes" with their potential for "threatening heroic song," since his lyre will allow him nothing but songs of love. (So lebt denn wohl, Heroen, / . . . Statt Heldensang zu drohen). He sounds genuinely grieved to leave off his heroic songs, and the wonderfully ominous rumble in the piano's bass on the word "drohen" (threatening) suggests that on the right day, this rhapsode can declaim heroic epic with the best of them.

William Shakespeare

Schubert's generation was the time of the great Shakespeare translations into German. Indeed, romanticism throughout much of Europe can be largely marked by the acceptance of Shakespeare (1564–1616) as one of the most universal authors, if not *the* most universal.

"Ständchen: Horch! horch! die Lerch'" (Serenade: Hark, Hark, the Lark), D. 889 (1826)

> *"Hark, hark! The lark at heaven's gate sings, and Phoebus 'gins arise. My lady sweet, arise!"*

This is the exquisite aubade from the late play *Cymbeline*. Schubert's music here is much earthier than the more ethereal effect of Shakespeare's words in the original. The idea of Phoebus Apollo's horses, which pull the sun through the heavens, suggested the galloping tune and accompaniment that pervade the work. The original setting, like the Shakespearean lyric, contains only one stanza; two others were added after Schubert's death. This is essentially a bonbon, and like all bonbons is best enjoyed in moderation, i.e., one lyric is better than three. Liszt made a popular virtuoso arrangement of this song (and many other Schubert lieder) for solo piano later in the century as part of his mission to disseminate Schubert's music.

"An Silvia" (To Sylvia), D. 891 (1826)

"Who is Sylvia, what is she that all the swains commend her?"

This song comes from what is probably Shakespeare's first comedy, *The Two Gentlemen of Verona*. This is no bonbon. Like "Ave Maria," this is a hymn of praise, though of a more secular kind, which strides with unflappable assurance. The little echo effect in the piano after the singer's phrases is an unforgettable touch. Reed says, "Its perfection of form and expression is absolute" (1985, 49).

Colly Cibber

Colly Cibber (1671–1757) was a famous comic actor and playwright of the English Restoration era who created an adaptation of Shakespeare's *Richard III* that held the stage in preference to the original for generations. A very weak poet, he nevertheless managed to become poet laureate and the butt of Alexander Pope's *The Dunciad*.

"Der blinde Knabe" (The Blind Boy), D. 833, translated by Craigher (1825)

"O tell me, friends, what is this thing called light? I'm glad with what God has given me, though I am only a poor blind boy."

This text is one of the more revoltingly bathetic in song literature, but one forgets this the instant the lied begins. The song's quality is mysteriously luminous, not unlike the B-flat Sonata, D. 960, whose key it shares. Reed observes, "The pianist's gently swaying semiquavers suggest . . . a kind of graceful uncertainty" (1985, 94). The piano figuration signals not only the careful tapping of the boy's walking stick but also something far more intangible, the boy's "inner life so full of smiles" (Mein innres Leben schön mir lacht), which inspired the composer in creating the nimbus of sound that envelops the protagonist. This song requires a singer of exceptional emotional honesty and is richly moving when performed well.

Sir Walter Scott

The Scottish romantic poet and novelist Sir Walter Scott (1771–1832) was hugely popular in Schubert's day and maintained a high reputation into the early twentieth century. This verse comes from his novel *The Lady of the Lake*, which Rossini utilized for his delightfully tuneful opera *La donna del lago*.

"Ave Maria" (often called "Ellens dritter Gesang" [Ellen's Third Song]), D. 839, translated by Adam Storck (1825)

> *"Ave Maria! Virgin mild! We will sleep safely till the dawn, no matter how cruel men can be. O Mother, hear a pleading child! Ave Maria!"*

This may be Schubert's most famous composition. For nearly two centuries, millions of people have been moved by this song in the many adaptations to which it has been subjected. Its melody is indestructible in its emotional power. The most chaste to the most emotive of performances can bring a great mass of people to tears. It is always refreshing to hear in the original setting, with the piano's harplike pillow of sound supporting the ardent vocal melody. Like Bach's "Jesu Joy of Man's Desiring," which in some ways its timeless motion suggests, it is part of the religious heritage of mankind. This song was among the hits of Schubert and Vogl's lieder tour of upper Austria in the summer of 1825, one of the happiest periods in Schubert's life. In a letter to his parents back in Vienna, Schubert wrote of the song, "There was a good deal of surprise [here] at my piety, which found expression in a Hymn to the Blessed Virgin, which seems to have moved all hearts and created quite a devotional atmosphere. I fancy that is because my religious feeling is never forced, and I never compose hymns or prayers of this sort unless

I am involuntarily overcome by a sense of devotion, and then the feeling is, as a rule, genuine and heartfelt" (Schubert 1970, 95–96).

Johann Gaudenz von Salis-Seewis

A member of the Swiss Guard, Johann Gaudenz von Salis-Seewis (1762–1834) managed to live out the French Revolution in Paris. He met Goethe and Schiller on a tour of Germany and himself left a legacy of early romantic poetry.

"Der Jüngling an der Quelle" (The Youth by the Spring), D. 300 (1815?)

> *"Quiet, pearling brook, whispering poplars; you'll wake up my love.*
> *I wanted to forget the prudish girl, but your leaves and the brook*
> *sigh out her name: Louise!"*

At first glance this is a commonplace lyric, but the music transforms it into something rich and strange. The slow motion of the pulse allows the piano's notes to cast a mysterious, opiatelike atmosphere over the singer's words. This song is a gentle soliloquy, half dreaming, half waking. The words that seemed such romantic commonplace suddenly become exquisitely beautiful. The hazy overlapping of the girl's name at the close haunts the ear long after the song is over.

Jacob Nicholaus Craigher de Jachelutta

A well-traveled, polyglot Italian, Jacob Nicholaus Craigher de Jachelutta (1797–1855) settled in Vienna and was associated with the Schlegel literary circle. He met Schubert and proposed translating poetry for the composer to set, as well as rendering Italian singing versions of some lieder. He is responsible for the Cibber translation above and was the poet of the following original lieder texts.

"Totengräbers Heimwehe" (Gravedigger's Longing), D. 842 (1825)

> *"O mankind—O life!—where's it all leading? Digging, burying, no stop for rest. What a wretched fate, I can't endure it. Life is stifling, the grave is so cool! But who will take me there? I stand alone by the edge of the grave, a cross in my hand. O homeland of peace, you beckon me from far off. My eyes close, I'm sinking! Loved ones, I come!"*

This through-composed song is one of the more powerful of Schubert's maturity. The oppressive rhythmic drive of the first section depicts the gravedigger's anguish and exhaustion. The piano seems to literally hammer away at him like necessity itself. His vocal phrases come out as gasps between the frequent rests punctuating his speech. The next section, where he laments his fate, carries the same unrelenting forward motion, but now the piano becomes softer while the singer's phrases become more connected and lyrical, as if a movie camera has moved in from an establishing shot to a close-up. "O Death, come and close (drücke) my eyes." The lovely ornament on "drücke" reveals all his "longing" for death and peace. This image beguiles the poor man into a moment of silence that marks the return of the implacable opening keyboard material, newly intensified by pounding triplets in the piano's bass.

A new fear enters the protagonist's mind: "Who will lay me in the grave? I'm all alone, completely alone!" (wer legt mich hinein?— / Ich stehe allein!—so ganz allein!). These fearful questions are broken by frightened pauses, like gasps of panic. Now the music transitions into a passage of bone-chilling stasis. "Abandoned by everyone, Death my only kin, I wait on the edge—the cross in my hand" (Von allen verlassen / Dem Tod nur verwandt, / Verweil' ich am Rande— / Das Kreuz in der Hand). This slow section, with its infinitely sad vocal melody deriving from the inflection of the words, is punctuated by uncanny trills in the pianist's right and left hands. The universal fear of death is distilled into about eight bars of indelible music. (Schubert himself knew how special this moment was, as it reappears in the opening movement of the A Minor Piano Sonata, D. 845, of the same year.)

But redemption is coming for this hapless loner as the piano performs another magical segue into new, slower, yet lighter textures. The staccato markings in the piano herald the singer's destination and he sings a new, gorgeous melody greeting this blessed land (Seligen Land). As the music becomes ever quieter, the singer's phrases begin to break up again with frequent rests. But now it is not from frustration or fear but rather a musical expression of the process of dying. He has just enough strength for one last lyrical outpouring of connected phrases, repeating over and over, "Dear ones, I come!" (Ihr Lieben— / Ich komme!). The accompaniment grows ever more ethereal, the voice ever softer as we are transported out of our world in much the same way the trills carry the variation theme into Elysium in the last movement of Beethoven's Sonata, Op. 111.

"Die junge Nonne" (The Young Nun), D. 828 (1824–25)
(CD Track 14)

> *"How the storm howls through the treetops! Not long ago life was raging inside me! Love flared like lightning, and my heart was as dark as the grave! In my heart there is peace and rest! I await you, my Savior, my Bridegroom! The bells toll peacefully in the tower. Hallelujah!"*

Craigher's poems are exercises in romantic sentimentalism. But Schubert has captured the dramatic interior and exterior worlds implicit in them to create works of transcendent dramatic and emotional power. Here is another of those songs that contain more drama than is found in many an opera. The nun's internal as well as external "storms" are unforgettably evoked in the awe-inspiring piano writing, which contains the tolling of the nunnery's bell tower from the very opening (0:04). Few composers are as adept at suggesting the dangers of nature and humankind's ambiguous relationship to it. The nun's opening lines (0:24) convey her dread at the storm's rage. The vocal monotone (0:56–1:17) on which she relates "And the night is dark as the grave!" (Und finster die Nacht, wie das Grab!) is musical-dramatic scene setting of the most blood-chilling order. To music veering unstably between minor and major, the nun confesses that "not long ago" (1:22) a similar storm raged within her, stirred by sexual passion. The music makes the listener question how well this inner storm has been quelled. Any doubts are resolved by the transition to the major key (2:20), which gives her vocal melody a sense of transcendence. It is one of the noblest of Schubert's themes. The storm may "rage on" because "in my heart is peace, in my heart is calm!" (Im Herzen ist Friede, im Herzen ist Ruh!).

She awaits her "Bridegroom" as a "loving bride purified by testing fire, wedded to eternal Love" (Des Bräutigams harret die liebende Braut, / Gereinigt in prüfender Glut— / Der ewigen Liebe getraut). The bright, cascading keyboard figurations (2:38–2:48) under the reference to the "testing fire" are sensually thrilling. The passion that so threatened the young woman outside the convent is sublimated in her religious fervor. A similarly swooning ecstasy is heard in the swelling phrase (2:58) "claim your bride!" (hole die Braut!), which anticipates Wagner in his more melodically expansive moments. After she asks for relief from her earthly bonds, the bell's tolling is brought into the foreground at last (3:13), both in her words and in the piano part as the inner and outer storms begin to recede. This "cross-fade" between the peaceful bell and the storm's rumbling, the storm threatening to return (3:46) and then ebbing into the background, is one of the miracles of music. The closing "Hallelujah!" (4:01), chanted above the ever-softening atmosphere of bell and wind, fearlessly unites the spiritual and sensual sides of this woman who has revealed her innermost soul to the audience in a space of some four or five minutes.

Four Special Songs

The four lieder discussed here are too beautiful and distinctive to leave out of any discussion of Schubert's songs, though they fall outside conventional art song boundaries. Several genres popular in Schubert's time on which the composer lavished some of his greatest music are encountered all too rarely in concert today. These include the masterpieces for piano four hands as well as the songs discussed in this chapter for glee clubs and concert songs with an instrumental soloist joining the singer and pianist. These "special songs" create vivid pictures and situations that hint at what Schubert could have achieved in opera had he found an excellent librettist and been blessed with a longer life.

Two Songs with Glee Clubs (Männerchor)

"Nachthelle" (Starry Night), D. 892, text by Seidl (1826)

> *In a romantic paean to the pure night sky and the glittering stars, the poet's heart is filled to "overflowing" with feelings of "freedom." The "bonds" of the world are no match for the feelings awakened by the radiant night.*

(See Chapter 5 for details on Seidl.)

"Nachthelle" was conceived for a tenor soloist, pianist, and men's chorus. Classified as one of Schubert's secular choral works, the song is a product of the Austrian-German tradition of amateur choruses so popular throughout the nineteenth century. The male glee club ensemble, or *Männerchor*, serves as backup to a tenor soloist and pianist, creating a kind of exploded lieder form. Along with the song "Nacht und Träume," "Nachthelle" is Schubert's greatest "night piece" and one of his most exhilarating and unforgettable creations.

The hushed, rapid pulsations that characterize the piano writing conjure a scene of the purest "silver" starlight bathing a town. The very houses seem spellbound by the flickering radiance. The workaday Biedermeier world is transfigured into a magical place of beauty and freedom. The tenor must possess an easy and comfortable high range and exemplary breath control if he is not to break the song's spell. "The night is clear and pure in brightest radiance" (Die Nacht ist heiter und ist rein, / Im allerhellsten Glanz). His hushed musical statements receive a gorgeous response from the choir, creating the musical illusion of height and depth that captures and ennobles Seidl's ideas. Much of the work is marked to be sung and played softly, suggesting the performers' hushed, quasi-religious reverence before this magical night scene. This makes the forceful setting of the last verses describing the poet's elation all the more overpowering. The tenor trades phrases back and forth with the choir, building to an orgiastic intensity on the words "[I feel] free and clear without any sorrow or anger" (frei und klar / Ganz ohne Leid und Groll). In the police state of Metternich's Vienna, such emotional experiences would indeed be hard to come by. The poet's insistence that his overflowing heart will break its bonds, "It's got to get out, it must get out" (Es will hinaus, es muss hinaus), creates a similar build through the excited interchanges of tenor and chorus until the song reaches a stunning climax as the soloist joins the chorus for a unison *fortissimo* statement proclaiming, "the last bonds break" (Die letzte Schranke bricht).

This peroration silences the voices, as if their and the listeners' souls have indeed broken the "surly bonds of earth," while the pianist begins a magical modulation back to the song's opening music. Much of the power of Schubert's music lies in his uncanny way of simply getting from one place to another, building tonal and emotional bridges where no other composer would have deemed it possible. This is one of the reasons Alfred Brendel has often characterized Schubert as "the sleepwalker" who miraculously skirts the edges of chaos and comes to a safe haven at last. Such alchemy leads to the song's recapitulation of the first verse, which Schubert treats to extended exploration, stopping time in its tracks. The coda starts with the basses alone beginning the final iterations of "Die Nacht ist heiter und ist rein." In an instant, all the voices are engaged with "im aller hellsten Glanz," sharing a diminuendo with the pianist, who allows the starry pulsations to fade back into the silence from which they emerged.

"Ständchen" (Serenade), D. 920, text: Grillparzer (1827)

> *"We've come here quietly to wake you with a gentle knock on the door. We call passionately, 'Don't sleep when the voice of affection speaks!' Once a wise man with a lantern searched far and wide for an honest man. It's rarer than gold to find people who really treasure us. Don't sleep when love speaks. But what is better than sleep? We'll softly steal away and end our happy song."*

Schubert titled several songs "Serenade," but this Grillparzer "Ständchen" occupies a place all its own. Franz Grillparzer (1791–1872), Austria's greatest playwright, had written the stirring funeral oration for Beethoven a few months before. An acquaintance of Schubert, he would be asked to compose the epitaph for his tomb. Composed on commission as a courtship gift for an acquaintance of the composer who was a relative of the poet, "Ständchen" was to be sung in a garden during a summer's night outside the beloved's window. The song calls for an alto soloist, a pianist, and a small chorus. One can imagine the young woman's surprise and delight at being awakened from sleep by the strains of this wonderful work. Secreting a pianoforte in a garden must have taken great ingenuity! Schubert's music captures and preserves the most ephemeral of moments: young people tiptoeing through the grass on a summer's night, the transition between innocence and experience, where, in Grillparzer's verse, "affection" (Neigung) dares to call itself "love" (Liebe). The music begins with a soft but nervously expectant portrayal of the assembling serenaders, presided over by the alto soloist's gentle but insistent directives. The second verse portrays the lover's emotions sublimated through the performers as the music begins building to a crescendo on repetitions of "rising, swelling, increasing" (steigend, schwellend, hebend). This viscerally erotic music finds its release in the powerful unison statements of "Don't sleep when affection calls to you!" (Schlaf' du nicht, / Wenn der Neigung Stimme spricht).

The idea of the wise Greek philosopher and the lantern at the start of the third verse inspires appropriately mock-serious counterpoint among chorus, soloist, and keyboard, a kind of Biedermeier version of Glenn Gould's delightful vocal ensemble, "So You Want to Write a Fugue?" But the tongue-in-cheek polyphony quickly vanishes and homophonic ardor returns at "when friendship, love itself speaks" (Drum wenn Freundschaft spricht, / Liebe spricht). "Love" is now traded back and forth between soloist and ensemble, leading to an apparent coda as the singers declare in a softly tapering phrase, "Don't sleep, dearest!" (Liebchen, schlaf' du nicht!). The piano effects a magical transition into a modified recapitulation of the opening material, as if the serenaders, their message delivered, recall where they are and begin their prolonged but graceful exit from the garden (apparently the pianist must fend for himself!). The long recapitulation allows the listener to savor the "happy tune" (frohe Weise) and the delicious textures and harmonies for a final time as they sing, "Softly, softly steal away!" (leise / Schleichen wir uns wieder fort!).

Two Songs with Obbligato Instruments

"Auf dem Strom" (On the River), D. 943, text: Rellstab (1828)

> *"Take these last good-bye kisses before you go. Already the boat's pulling away on the current. See how fast it all flies by! The river bears me steadily to the ocean. If I can't make out the shore I'll look up to the stars. By starlight I first called her mine; maybe there I'll see her face again."*

(See Chapter 10 on the *Schwanengesang* cycle for details on Rellstab.)

"Auf dem Strom" was written specially for the first and only public concert devoted solely to Schubert's works during his lifetime, given on March 26, 1828. A friend of the composer was a virtuoso horn player, and the idea of a lied including an extra instrumental partner would have seemed natural in the slightly grander milieu of a concert hall. Some commentators interpret "Auf dem Strom" as a memorial to Beethoven, who had died a year before. One theme, which is first heard setting the words "And so the waves carry me away" (Und so trägt mich denn die Welle), resembles a theme from the Funeral March in Beethoven's Eroica Symphony. All the same, the poem fits Schubert's concerns perfectly, and the alleged melodic quotation is hard to detect in its context even when someone is listening for it. "Auf dem Strom" is a glowing autumnal masterpiece treating the theme of death and departure.

The long prelude juxtaposes the keyboard's wavelike motif against the horn's slower, more expansive melody. The horn recalls the open Austrian countryside and creates the illusion of vast physical and spiritual spaces being traversed by the poem's protagonist. (One may remember the horn passage that opens Schubert's Great C Major Symphony.) The tenor's main theme is one of tender major-keyed wistfulness, frequently interrupted by threatening minor-key phrases representing some fateful imperative. Schubert's wonderfully expansive "Klavierstück," D. 946, no. 2, written at virtually the same time as this song, is similar with its barcarolle-like main theme and the darkly passionate "aquatic" turbulence that emerges in the piece's episodes. The final verse wherein the hero seeks his love's "glance" in the starry sky is lavishly developed. It is first set to the main theme before Schubert magically introduces a new melody that moves up and down the stave, imparting a feeling of hard-won grace. The long coda brings the three performers to a place of heavenly, mysterious peace.

As in *Winterreise*, the reasons for the singer's departure are unclear. The protagonist in "Auf dem Strom" has found both faithful love and a homeland; he's triumphed where most Schubertian subjects have failed. But now he must leave forever on a riverboat heading to the ocean (Weltmeer), a dark, cold place of storms where "no song can greet him" from home. Clearly the journey of Schubert's remarkably grounded hero is the one toward death that we all face; Hamlet's "undiscovered country from whose bourn / No traveler returns." In this sense, all mankind are wanderers. Yet despite the terrors of the unknown, this wanderer finds peace.

"Der Hirt auf dem Felsen" (The Shepherd on the Rock), D. 965, text: Müller/Chézy (1828)

> *"When I stand on the highest rock, looking down into the deep valley, the echo rises into the distance. My beloved lives so far from me; I long so much for her. I'm very sad; joy has left me. The spring will come, spring is my friend, and I shall be ready to go wandering."*

Finished only a month before Schubert's death, this song was created for a singer the composer had revered since he was sixteen, the prima donna Anna Milder-Hauptmann. In 1813 Schubert heard her sing the lead in Gluck's *Iphigénie en Tauride* with Vogl as Orest. This was one of the formative aesthetic experiences of his life. Others admired the singer as well. Beethoven's Leonora was created for her. Like her costar Vogl, Milder-Hauptmann came to love Schubert's music and wanted to find ways of promoting it. She had asked him for an extended concert piece with contrasts and great virtuosity. It took three years for Schubert to get around to finishing the work. The text is a clever composite of poetry he took from Wilhelm Müller, the author of Schubert's first two song cycles (see chapters 8 and 9), and a passage by Wihelmina von Chézy (1783–1856), the author of *Rosamunde*, the play for which he had written incidental music five years earlier. The clarinet obbligato part may have been inspired by a similar device in the aria "Parto, Parto" from Mozart's last opera, *La clemenza di Tito*.

"Der Hirt auf dem Felsen" fulfills every one of the prima donna's requests and represents a full-fledged operatic scene. The extensive prelude by the piano and clarinet creates the picturesque alpine setting, hinting at the presence of vast height, distance, and depth as well as the darker energies that lie beneath even the most ostensibly innocent of Schubert's music. The soprano plays a male character, as in several Rossini opera seria. His/her music contains the melodic charm and memorability of Rossini's most fetching tunes, allowing the voice and the clarinet obbligato to exhibit wonderful bravura. The yodeling in the music is quite delightful local color, especially when it is shared between the voice and piano.

The song's middle section portrays more serious emotions, reaching its climax in the shepherd's assertion that his song has "drawn hearts toward heaven with its miraculous power" (Die Herzen es zum Himmel zieht / Mit wunderbarer Macht), one of Schubert's last invocations of his life's work. An instrumental modulation changes the scene back to clear sunlight as the clarinet performs a deliciously theatrical, bird-like trill heralding spring. An allegretto caballetta section anticipating the coming of spring (Der Frühling will kommen) imparts a sense of unbuttoned joy as the work closes. In "Der Hirt" Schubert writes in a broader, more "public" voice for the song's intended concert hall audience, yet the song never disintegrates into banality. "Der Hirt" represents the composer at the end bestowing a rich gift on an artist who had profoundly impressed upon him the power that resides in music and words when they are combined with integrity by a composer and a performer.

Die Schöne Müllerin

"I can neither play nor sing, yet when I write verses, I sing and play after all. If I could produce the melodies, my songs would be more pleasing than they are now. But courage! Perhaps there is a kindred spirit somewhere who will hear the tunes behind the words and give them back to me." (an entry in Wilhelm Müller's diary, cited by Youens 1992, 10)

Wilhelm Müller (1794–1827) was a poet, teacher, and philologist who served as a privy councilor in Dessau, Germany, where he spent much of his life. Müller fought against Napoleon before dedicating himself to literature. His enthusiasm for Hellenic civilization and Greek independence from Turkish tyranny led to his nickname "Grieschen-Müller," i.e., Müller the Greek. Müller's extraordinary literary talent is manifest in the two poetic cycles, *Die Schöne Müllerin* and *Winterreise*, that Schubert set in 1823 and 1827. Read without the music they inspired, they reveal one of the more original of the romantics. Müller's work anticipates by several years Georg Büchner's (1814–37) insight into psychosis found in his plays and prose. Heinrich Heine greatly admired Müller's poetry, telling him, "How pure and clear your songs are—folksongs every one" (Stokes 2005, 349). Like Heine's, Müller's poems often posses a cryptic, mysterious narrative, sometimes ending in a line of biting, unexpected irony.

Sadly, Müller appears never to have met or been aware of Schubert. They led contrasting lives. While both artists died tragically young, Müller had a far happier personal life with a wife and children.

Nevertheless, his remark quoted above suggests that he found his poetic work only half finished without music to give it the fullest expression. Schubert, his personal life unstable and marred by chronic illness, managed to fulfill Müller's wish. Müller died unexpectedly in his sleep of a heart attack, aged thirty-three, the same year Schubert wrestled with his second and last Müller cycle, *Winterreise*.

The *Die Schöne Müllerin* poems were published in 1821. They tell the story of a hapless miller boy and his fatal obsession with the unattainable miller's daughter. When Müller published the poems he created an ironic framework including a prologue and epilogue (not set by Schubert) that warns the audience to view the story of a broken heart from an emotional distance. This is a ploy on Müller's part to deflect the autobiographical nature of the miller's (*Müller* in German) love and sorrow. Müller the poet had been romantically fixated on a young woman whom he lacked the courage to court. Unlike his alter ego, the real-life Müller was able to move on from his experience of unrequited love, but not before he had created the inspiration for what is arguably the greatest artistic representation of that universal experience.

It is unknown exactly how Schubert discovered this poetry cycle in early 1823. Schubert was always interested in large-scale forms, for all his genius at creating miniatures. Müller's cycle represents a first-person narrative, ideal for creating the kind of monodrama implicit in a connected song cycle. Beethoven's much briefer *An die ferne Geliebte* was the only model for a lieder cycle. By 1823, Schubert's compositional mastery made him ready to challenge and completely surpass Beethoven's example. Just as importantly, the plight of Müller's miller would have had a deep emotional resonance for the composer. He too had relinquished the one serious love of his life, Therese Grob, several years before, for far more tangible financial and sociological reasons than those blocking the miller from his goal. By the time he began the composition, Schubert knew he had a venereal disease that could easily lead to madness before it claimed his life. In Müller's cycle he saw a reflection of himself in the brook's waters, just as clearly as the poet had a few years before and had so transparently attempted to conceal through the ironic prologue and epilogue, which Schubert rightly omits.

So much again for the "naive" composer unable to detect that *Die Schöne Müllerin* was some sort of stylized put-on. Schubert, especially now, had an unerring ability to detect human suffering. He homed in on the essential nature of what Müller had created, understanding him better than Müller understood himself. By musically dramatizing the miller boy's journey from youthful innocence to acutely painful erotic experience and his eventual self-destruction in the brook, Schubert faced down his own demons, framing them into art. The suicidal boy's death in a sense allowed Schubert to live on into a very uncertain future. As Johnson observes, "If listening to music can change a life, how much more true must that be for the person writing it" (Johnson 1989–97, 25: 70). A similar artistic transference would occur four years later when Schubert discovered Müller's *Winterreise*.

Die Schöne Müllerin is not, however, merely a dry run for *Winterreise*. It is a towering masterpiece, which is all the more startling when one considers its absolute originality. Objectively speaking, *Die Schöne Müllerin* is every bit as deep as its winter companion. It is mainly the pervasive nihilism of the late twentieth and early twenty-first centuries that privilege the later masterpiece over the earlier one. But performers such as Brigitte Fassbaender have testified that the earlier cycle's emotional extremes are even harder to realize than *Winterreise* (1995, 2).

At first encounter, it may seem a lopsided piece, thirteen "happy" songs followed by seven "tragic" ones. But the so-called "happy" songs are clouded with intimations of disaster, especially the miller's propensity for hallucination and longing for self-destruction. In fact, the first thirteen songs contain elements often more disturbing than the more obvious horrors of *Winterreise*. Schubert's earlier exploration of Mayrhofer's psychological obsessions and his own condition at the time would have provided all the understanding he needed of the miller boy's experience: a world of uniquely personal color and beauty shot through with an awareness of pain that only this composer could render in music. Van Gogh's exploration of his world generations later offers a distant but instructive artistic parallel.

The completed cycle of twenty lieder (D. 795) was published as Opus 25 in five distinct books or sets during 1824. Maurice Brown suggests that these five sets of songs each "make some attempt to present the five small 'Acts' of the [*Müllerin*] play: I—the arrival at the mill ([songs] 1–4), II—the falling in love (5–9), III—the brief idyll of happiness (10–13), IV—the jealousy and despair (14–17), V—the resignation and death of the young miller (18–20)" (Brown 1958, 152). Brown's idea may be helpful in encountering *Die Schöne Müllerin* for the first time and is incorporated here.

Act One: The Arrival at the Mill

"Das Wandern" (Wandering)

"Wandering is the miller's happiness and way of life."

The bumptious piano prelude calls the cycle's protagonist before our imagination. His first lied could easily be a folk song or a ditty he has invented to sing as he wanders the countryside looking for work, leaving his apprenticeship to seek new horizons. Many Schubert songs deal with wandering and restlessness. In this one, humankind's transitory position in the romantic universe is at its most happy and exuberant. The miller, like all good romantics, intuits a unity between himself and nature, especially the water, which makes everything from mill wheels to millstones move in a merry dance of perpetual motion. How perfectly Schubert's strophic music is tailored to fit each of the song's verses! Good performers will sculpt the same notes for voice and keyboard to create the images of the happy young man's eager footsteps, the rushing stream waters, the rotation of the wheels, the endearingly clumsy millstones trying so hard to dance (Sie tanzen mit den muntern Reihn), returning to the miller at his moment of optimistic departure into the wide world. Seen from the perspective of the song cycle as a whole, this widely adaptable opening music suggests a great deal of the miller's personality—his idealism as well as the emotional and imaginative sensitivities that lead him to anthropomorphize his environment, which will bring him both ecstasy and sorrow as the drama develops.

"Wohin?" (Where Are You Leading Me?) (CD Track 15)

"I can hear the gurgling of a little stream as it rushes down into the valley. I had to follow it, for mill wheels turn by every clear stream!"

Here is some of Schubert's finest water music to introduce the character of the particular brook that leads the miller to his destiny. This song is often detached and sung apart from the other *Müllerin* songs in recital. The melody is one of Schubert's most memorable, and the song's seeming artlessness makes its popularity easy to understand. But the artlessness is only apparent. This is one of the subtlest songs in the entire literature, a constantly changing through-composed song that hypnotizes the listener into believing that it is a strophic song, just as the singing of the water nymphs hypnotizes the miller.

The steady gurgling of the stream sounds in the keyboard as the miller's voice floats over it, singing one of Schubert's most beautiful melodies, suffused with sunlit radiance. The tonality darkens for only a moment (0:18) as the miller sings, "I don't know why, or what made me, or who put the thought in my head" (Ich weiss nicht, wie mir wurde, / Nicht, wer den Rat mir gab). But the brook's major-key radiance instantly reasserts itself (0:26), luring the miller onward. His next verse, "I keep going downward" (Hinunter und immer weiter), finds the keyboard's bass adding glowing resonance (0:41) to the sonority; maybe the miller is close enough to look into the water's depths that will prove so fateful in the story's outcome? The crescendo in the accompaniment reaches its crest and the keyboard-water suddenly grows quieter (1:04) as he asks a pregnant question, "Is this my path then?" (Ist dass denn meine Strasse?). The lyrical flow of vocal melody becomes more speechlike. A good interpreter, like Hermann Prey, manages to let this question hang in the air without compromising the song's onward, waterlike movement. "Oh, little brook, say where you're leading? Where? Say where you're leading?" (O Bächlein, sprich, wohin? Wohin? Sprich wohin?). The repetitions (1:10–1:17) are Schubert's, highlighting the song's moment of dramatic recognition. The miller divines that his fate hangs in the balance.

"You have with your rustling quite taken over my mind" (Du hast mit deinem Rauschen / Mir ganz berauscht den Sinn). These words, the first hint of the miller's unorthodox, perhaps unhealthy turn of mind, is set to a sudden burst of rich minor-key melody from both voice and piano (1:17–1:32). The brook's path will indeed lead to madness, literally a "rustling of [his] whole mind" (mir ganz berauscht den Sinn). But rather than break free of the watery lure, he identifies the "rustling" to be "the singing and dancing of the water nymphs deep below" (Es singen wohl die Nixen / Tief unter ihren Reihn). Supernatural water nymphs have a nasty habit of dragging besotted young men into the depths throughout European folklore, but these words about the "Nixen" (1:40) are sung to the sunny melody of the opening verse. The miller's music implies he is trapped in his own subjective world, singing what will prove the most foreboding of words to the strains of the song's opening. He is doomed by his tragic misapprehension of his surroundings. "Let them sing, lad, and the water rustle" (Lass singen, Gesell, lass rauschen), he joyfully proclaims (1:55) to music with just the hint of darker tonality. The fleeting moment of tragic presentment is pushed aside, the miller remembers his calling, and the tragedy begins to unfold under the broad sunshine of the closing music. "Where there's a clear stream you can count on a mill wheel turning."

"Halt!" (Stop!)

> *"I see a mill gleaming among the alder trees. Dear brooklet, is this what you meant?"*

The whirling mill wheel sounds in the rolling arpeggio and the water, tamed by the heavy wheel, courses evenly in the piano figuration. Once established, the wheel and water sounds become delightful background scenery for the miller's soliloquy as he stands rapt before the mill. His joy reaches exultation and his voice climbs thrillingly above the stave as he describes the sun shining over the scene (Und die Sonne, wie helle / Vom Himmel sie scheint!). He asks the brook, "Was this what you meant?" (War es also gemeint?). This last phrase is repeated by Schubert three times until the song and the water's movement fade in diminuendo. Each iteration of the word "this" (also) is treated to a similar languishing figuration. The shift from his ecstatic paean to the sun to the obsessive question at the song's end reveals Schubert already sculpting the miller's personality. The music is subtly portraying a passionate, unstable figure before the "maid of the mill," let alone the hunter, appears. The bright sun and clear water of this music reflects much more than the naive nature painting that listeners of an older generation tended to hear.

"Danksagung an den Bach" (Thanksgiving to the Brook)

> *"Is this what you meant, babbling friend? 'To the girl of the mill!'*
> *I asked for work, now I've got enough for both my hands and my*
> *heart!"*

The miller boy contemplates the beautiful miller's daughter for the first time in this gorgeous ABA song. The keyboard drones a lullabylike prelude that forms the basis for the song's accompaniment in gentle 2/4 time. It is as if the brook's flow has pointedly slowed down as the young man approaches his destined love. At least this is how the miller boy perceives it. He senses nature's mysterious participation in all of his emotional life. But as in great tragedy, the miller boy is incapable of reading nature's seemingly simple signs. "Is this what you meant, my babbling friend?" (War es also gemeint, / Mein rauschender Freund?) is set suggestively. The reference to the "babbling friend" has a gently rising wave pattern in the vocal line, while "War es also gemeint" rises in intensity and pitch to a high G on "gemeint." This is the highest note in the song and is used to accent other words with passionate urgency. At the first mention of the old miller's daughter, in the phrase "Zur Müllerin hin" (to the girl of the mill), the note helps to add an erotic charge to the caressing figure that decorates her name. The intensity of the music tells us a fantasy is being formed that cannot be dislodged.

The next verse transposes the melody into the minor with all of Schubert's characteristic alchemy. This modulation brings us deeper into the boy's consciousness as he perceives an uncanny mystery lying beneath the surface of things. He asks the brook, "Did she send you

herself?" (Hat sie dich geschickt?). "A delicate figure in the bass . . .
replies in the minor, but the boy ignores this, finding his own way
back to his G major," observes Fischer-Dieskau (1978, 178). The two
repetitions of this question have a strangely insistent F-natural on each
mention of the girl (sie). The music, taking its cue from the poetry,
captures the very moment when the boy's adolescent daydreaming
begins to become dangerously solipsistic. "I accept my fate" (Ich gebe
mich drein) receives the same, slightly uncanny F-natural on "gebe."
The world is as the miller wishes it to be, however much he says the
truth doesn't matter. Half a bar of solo keyboard brings us back to a
recapitulation of the song's opening melody as the miller boy revels in
his apparent fulfillment, with "enough" work for his hands and heart.
The high note used earlier on "gemeint" returns on the second syllable
of "genug" (enough), signaling that the cycle's emotional journey has
reached its first important station. Schubert's "first act" ends on a point
of premature calm.

Act Two: Falling in Love

"Am Feierabend" (After Work)

> *"If I had a hundred arms to keep the wheels roaring on my own,
> then the beautiful girl of the mill would see my sincerity! But I'm
> too weak! In the after hours, the master speaks to us all, "I'm
> pleased with your work," and the dear girl says, "Everyone have a
> good night."*

The song's title, suggestive of relaxation, and the lulling music of the
preceding song make the prelude of "Am Feierabend" all the more surprising. The strong, rapid chords with their sharp accents are followed
by the nervous, flowing watery pattern that will make up much of the
accompaniment. The music is a representation of erotic and spiritual
frustration. The reference to the "Müllerin" is set to high-lying vocal
declamation; the boy's professed "sincerity" (treuen) to a luxuriant
decoration all its own. The turbulent millstream water shifts back to the

almost spastic chords of the opening measures as the miller boy sings his frustration about his "weakness" (so schwach) to short-breathed anxious phrases, a physical enactment of his impotence in the presence of the faceless fellow workers who surround him. In less than a measure and with the help of a lulling trill from the piano, we are brought directly into the boy's present reality. He is sitting in a "big circle" (grossen Runde) in the ostensibly restful hours after work—what has gone before was all a product of his increasingly feverish sensibility.

"The master speaks to us all" (Und der Meister spricht zu Allen) is sung almost entirely to a droning F that embodies the old miller's tiredness at day's end as well as the narrating miller boy's frustration that the words will be for "Allen" and not for him alone. "I'm pleased with your work" (Euer Werk hat mir gefallen) are the first words we've heard from anyone other than the boy. The music, which affords the singer an opportunity to enact the older man for this one moment in the cycle, has a lyrical, kindly rise and fall. The by-rote textual and musical repetition, however, reminds the young miller of his failure to distinguish himself from his fellows. One greeting fits all. "And the dear girl says" (Und das liebe Mädchen sagt) is sung to a slightly more varied drone that lifts the voice naturally higher to begin the brief representation of the girl. "Everyone have a good night" (Allen eine gute Nacht). Her words are instantly repeated like the master's words had been. The high Gs on "Allen" are physically lovely in their delicate suggestion of her femininity and emotionally piercing for the boy. Again he is reminded that he is just one of a group. Both the father's and daughter's recollected speech is sung over static chords that hang in the air. The "memory chords" effectively block out external distraction so he can fruitlessly parse the words again and again.

His frustration boils over into an even faster reprise of the opening. The coda is electrifying. The rapid movement of both voice and piano is abruptly arrested for the final repetitions of "Dass die schöne Müllerin" (that the beautiful girl of the mill) and "Merkte meinen treuen Sinn!" (would see my sincerity), each sung as if in suspended animation to the "memory chords," the rushing keyboard writing violently bursting out between the phrases. Two angry chords end the song. Schubert has found musically and dramatically innovative ways to articulate his protagonist's inner and outer worlds. It is hard to think of any opera composers before Schubert's time, except Monteverdi and Mozart, whose work could offer comparable depth of characterization and psychological insight.

"Der Neugierige" (The Questioner)

"I can't ask a flower or star; none can tell me what I want to hear. O brooklet of my love, how mysterious you are! Say, does she love me?"

Fresh from the feverish pace of "Am Feierabend," the miller seems now to have all the time in the world to contemplate his love and build his unmatchable expectations. The song's structure is unusual: AABC (recitative) B. The A section is made up of a tender, hesitant melody as the miller, in his self-imposed loneliness, seeks a (typically) insentient confidant. The frequent vocal rests suggest his timidity and extreme vulnerability, all reflected in the tender questioning of the keyboard writing. The B section, marked "very slow," literally opens the floodgates to the brooklet, the miller's only true friend. The gentle water laps in the keyboard beneath a vocal melody of piercing tenderness, "O brooklet of my love" (O Bächlein meiner Liebe). The tonality hints eerily at the minor as the miller remarks, "How silent you are today!" (Wie bist du heut' so stumm!). Even at its most placid flowing, Schubert's music hints at a nameless danger that lurks in the seemingly "friendly brook." The stream's waters in the piano modulate to a passage of recitative. "'Yes' is one word, the other is 'no'" (Ja, heisst das eine Wörtchen, / Dass andre heisset Nein). The keyboard changes from flowing watery semiquavers to simple underpinning chords for this speechlike declamation. It is as if, in John Reed's words, "we switch into a close up" (1985, 185). The miller's "whole world" rests on the answer to this ultimate question, "Does she love me or not?" and only the conversational declamation of recitative can express such a quandary. Chordal patterns of magical ambiguity assert themselves in the piano as the miller weighs "the two words" in which his "whole world is enclosed" (Die beiden

Wörtchen schliessen / Die ganze Welt mir ein). Seldom has emotional vulnerability been expressed so penetratingly as here. The return to the flowing B section for the final verse is all the more poignant after what has gone before. The voice's flirtation with the minor key on "how wonderfully mysterious you are!" (Was bist du wunderlich!) strikes the ear even more uncannily than before. The brook-piano continues its mellifluous way for several bars after the miller stops singing, as if seeking a resolution that never comes.

"Ungeduld" (Impatience)

"I'd like to carve it everywhere: 'My heart is yours, and always will be.' She doesn't see any of these frightening urges."

This strophic song is the most famous number in *Die Schöne Müllerin*, frequently performed outside of the cycle. The powerful, ringing declamation "My heart is yours, and always will be!" (Dein ist mein Herz, und soll es ewig bleiben!) makes it a very attractive display piece for a strong tenor voice. Out of context and falsely utilized as a virtuoso display piece, it becomes a kind of drawing-room version of Siegfried's forging song. But the text alone should alert the reader that this is no conventional love song. Such songs don't progress from alerting all of inanimate nature to the depths of one's passion while saving for the final two lines the fact that "she doesn't see any of these frightening urges" (bangen Trieben) surging through him. The music too hints that something is amiss. The voice seems slightly out of synch with the piano until the declaration "Dein ist mein Herz," which closes each verse. The singer is overwhelmed with emotion, which threatens his ability to follow the music's beat. Ironically, the hard-won unity between voice and accompaniment at this point, what most of us would consider the norm in a love song, becomes unsettling in its near maniacal certitude. During the prelude the pianist has an awkward climbing melodic figure in the bass that seems to comment ironically on the other hand's steady pulse of excited semiquavers and the miller's pathetically misplaced exhilaration.

"Morgengruss" (Morning Greeting)

"Good morning, beautiful miller girl! Why do you turn away as if something is bothering you? Then I'll go away."

The miller's words give us fleeting glimpses of the world surrounding him. The poor girl is seemingly uneasy with his attentions. Unable to take a hint, he promises to keep his distance by watching her window from afar. One hopes for the girl's sake the text is only an inner monologue. In modern terms, we seem to be entering restraining-order territory, but this is not the direction in which either Schubert or the poet is aiming. Some of the earlier songs strongly depict the boy's severe emotional instability. But the miller boy, more at home with inanimate nature than other human beings and clueless with regard to the girl's signals, would not hurt a fly, and Schubert's music makes this abundantly clear. C major often signals images of radiance and light. The music is like a folk song. The "moderate" tempo keeps the song from dragging or prematurely exaggerating the miller boy's pathology. The glowing melody suggests the boy's bigness of heart. The core of the whole setting lies in the last verse, with its evocation of the lark, the sky, and "God's bright morning" (Gottes hellen Morgen), sung over the piano's even-flowing triplets. In romantic thought, such obvious reverence for nature signals the innate goodness of the observer.

"Des Müllers Blumen" (The Miller's Flowers)

"The blue flowers by the brook are like my sweetheart's eyes—that makes them my flowers."

Here is another strophic setting of folklike simplicity. A sweet melody graces the poet's images of "bright blue eyes and flowers," and the friendly brook's presence is suggested in the piano's flowing triplets. The only suggestion of disharmony is the strangely solitary chord struck softly in the bass of the keyboard at the start of the prelude— a momentary warning of the danger that lies deep in the stream and deep beneath the seemingly carefree beauty of this song.

"Tränenregen" (Raining Tears)

"We sat so intimately together, gazing down into the stream. The moon had come out, and the stars. I gazed only at her reflection. It seemed the sky had sunk into the brook, and the brook called after me: 'Friend, follow me.' My eyes watered, the mirror blurred; she said: 'It's going to rain; good-bye, I'm going home.'"

This song is the lynchpin of the whole cycle, allowing us to see the protagonist at a crossroads. The last word of the previous song was "weeping," and this song seems to instantly deliver on that promise (Johnson 1989–97, 25: 32). The piano prelude that sounds before each of the first three verses captures the ambiguity of the scene. The prelude presents a struggle to find a steady mood, of sadness or of happiness, the right hand striving upward while the bass counterpoint pulls downward. It is like the rippling surface of the brook changing from a clear to a blurred reflection, or the emotional sensation of attempting to hold back tears. Somehow the miller has finessed, or more likely stumbled onto, a moment alone with the girl in the most romantic of settings. At the midpoint of each verse, as the singer's voice comes to a rest, the keyboard-brook gurgles in its most alluring way, helping to paint a scene of what should be perfect bliss.

One might expect the miller to try to talk to her or even to kiss her if they are bonded as closely as his words imply. Instead he is tellingly absorbed with looking not at her but at her reflection in the water and the flowers that he thinks reflect the color of her eyes. We are left to imagine what the girl is experiencing as the boy begins hallucinating that the heavens have been drawn under water and the brook begins directly to lure him into its depths. As the brook renews its pleasing sounds in the keyboard, unsettling irony manifests. The lovely sounds we and the girl are hearing delight the ear and paint lovely pictures. The boy is hearing something quite different: a voice from nature calling him to his death. The key shifts suddenly to the minor for the last verse, marking the boy's moment of recognition that death is summoning him in a form more alluring than even the miller girl could ever be. His tears cloud his vision and disturb the clear reflection of the brook. Perhaps the girl has been equally entranced by the brook's reflection and sees the teardrops as the beginning of rain. Maybe rain really is coming. Or perhaps she senses there is something not quite right with the boy and wants to make as polite an exit as possible. "It's going to rain; good-bye, I'm going home" (Es kommt ein Regen, / Ade, ich geh' nach Haus), she sings, through the miller's voice, her music in the major key of the earlier verses, their emotional incompatibility expressed by the banality of the words and the simple clash of major and minor. The piano's postlude repeats the placid yet tonally unstable music of the prelude. Is it an indication of his sadness at her departure or of his continued obsession with what the millstream is saying to him? The danger the water represents has revealed itself. The cycle's real action has finally become clear. Eros (erotic love) and thanatos (death) are reaching for the soul of the protagonist. This song may represent the first significant portrayal of schizophrenia in art.

Act Three: Happiness

"Mein!" (Mine!)

> *"Brooklet, stop your gurgling! Mill wheels, cease your noise! The beloved mill girl is mine! Mine!"*

This is another famous song that loses its disturbing undercurrents when performed out of context. The psychological disconnect between the last song and this one is very jarring. "Tränenregen" not only hints at the distance between the miller and the girl but also leaves an even stronger impression of the miller's suicidal longings and encroaching insanity. Whatever has triggered his current mood of manic joy is known only to him. The song is in ABA structure. The piano proclaims a joyous prelude that recalls something of the feelings and sounds of the first song of the cycle. One can imagine the mill wheels grinding merrily in the (keyboard) background as the boy proclaims his imagined triumph. The melodic movement of his voice, almost yodeling in his delight, hints at some of the first song's characteristic up-and-down patterns. The music suggests that the miller has found his ultimate home, the "hand"

and "heart" work that will give him fulfillment. The proclamation "The beloved miller girl is mine!" (Die geliebte Müllerin ist mein!) is treated to a ringing declamation by voice and piano that almost puts "Dein ist mein Herz" from "Ungeduld" in the shade.

The B section beginning with "Spring, haven't you any more flowers?" (Frühling, sind das alle deine Blümelein?) intensifies the happy mood. Disappointed by nature's failure to celebrate his fortune, the miller expresses resignation at having "to be all alone with the happy word 'mine,' not understood in all of creation" (so muss ich ganz allein, / Mit dem seligen Worte mein, / Unverstanden in der weiten Schöpfung sein). Again he reveals a glimpse of the reality of his loneliness, yet the music gives only the smallest hints of minor tonality in the setting of this line. The elaboration given "unverstanden" (not understood) on its two appearances suggests the miller is practically luxuriating in his singularity. It is telling also that the girl is reduced to an abstract concept, "my happy word," rather than enjoying real human status. The resurgent A section brings the song to its close, the always emotionally enabling accompaniment proclaiming the "victory" in a triumphant postlude.

"Pause" (Time Out)

> "I've hung my lute on the wall and tied a green ribbon around it.
> I can't sing anymore, my heart is too full. If a breeze moves across
> your strings, is it the prelude to new songs?"

Throughout much of the song, the piano imitates the strumming of the miller on his lute, or rather the miller's memory of his own playing, since, as he tells us, he cannot make any more music for the moment; his heart is too full of joy. Throughout the "remembered" lute playing in the accompaniment we can recognize the breaks and discontinuities of instrumental improvisations. His first vocal melody breathes contentment and his pleasure is palpable on the lovely ornament given "grünen" (green), the color of the ribbon with which he adorns his instrument and that will figure importantly later in the cycle. Green can symbolize innocence and youth but also fecundity and nature itself.

The second section in a startling minor key expresses "the burning pain of my longing I could put into playful song" (Meiner Sehnsucht allerheissesten Schmerz / Durft' ich aushauchen in Liederscherz). How quickly the miller's mood can change at the drop of a measure! Equally without warning, lyric vocal music turns to recitative sung startlingly to the piano's *più forte* chords. "Ah, how great my happiness is that no sound on earth can contain it" (Ei, wie gross ist wohl meines Glückes Last, / Dass kein Klang auf Erden es in sich fasst?). How odd to sing of happiness in recitative that seems so readily susceptible to the pull of the minor! After a bar and a half of accompanimental uncertainty, the prelude's strumming resumes.

The miller muses that a breeze or a bee could happen to touch the strings and create the kind of "chance" music in which romantics from Coleridge to Goethe took such an interest, i.e., the so-called aeolian harp. His vocal melody changes into recitative when he imagines this phenomenon: "I will be so afraid and shudder" (Da wird mir so bange und es durchschauert mich). The setting of "shudder" (durchschauert) is a short but wrenching dissonance followed by a bar's rest for the singer. The boy's happiness literally rests as precariously as the winds blow (an anticipation of the song "Letzte Hoffnung" in *Winterreise*).

While he is alone within his own thoughts, the memory of his strumming lute returns, encouraging him back to lyrical song as he frets over the ribbon's position on the lute. "It often flies across the strings with a soft sound." The piano-lute strums a measure-long variant in a minor key, the chance music that so perplexes him, as the boy formulates two questions that will constitute the song's final surprise: "Is this the echo of my love pain? Or is it the prelude to new songs?" (Ist es der Nachklang meiner Liebespein? / Soll es das Vorspiel neuer Lieder sein?). The vocal music transforms yet again, this time into a kind of arioso or lyrical recitative. A good performer makes these words sound like they are directly addressing the audience with the most urgent question in the world. Hesitantly, the piano-lute repeats its soloistic questioning. The singer repeats his question; his whole world, as he well knows, is his to lose. The piano strums its coda, punctuated by two pregnant pauses, before the song comes to its rest. John Reed thought this "the most subtle and inspired song in the cycle" (1985, 188).

"Mit dem grünen Lautenbande" (With the Green Lute Ribbon)

" 'It's too bad this lovely green ribbon should fade here on the wall,
I like green so much!' That's what you said to me today, dear; I've
untied it and sent it to you; now enjoy the green!"

This is the last of the "happy" songs and the most carefree song of the cycle. The miller's and the audience's guard is down and all the more unprepared for the tragic reversal about to occur. Gerald Moore observes, "Every phrase in this dear little song is fragrant with happiness" (1975, 43). This is music of irreducible purity. The way the pianist's right hand travels high above the stave to double the voice during the close of each verse is particularly lovable. Somehow the girl has been in the miller's room, or at least looked in the door. Her innocuous remark leads to the mawkish delivery of a (symbolically) faded ribbon. Never since the handkerchief in Shakespeare's *Othello* or Verdi's opera has an innocent textile been given such dangerous significance. The miller's use of "we" and "our" (wir, unser) is a pathetic touch. Also potentially ominous is the information that the girl's self-professed lover wears "all white" (Ist auch dein ganzer Liebster weiss). Superficially he is referring to the mill flour that is the product of his work. But like the idea of green, whiteness will take on a metaphoric life of its own. This sense of whiteness comprises innocence, pale shock, and death itself. All these disturbing elements flow unchecked in the lovely music. Why shouldn't they? They are all natural and beautiful to the miller's mind, and that is tragically his only reality.

Act Four: Jealousy and Despair

"Der Jäger" (The Hunter)

"What's the hunter want by the millstream here? Stay away, you
arrogant hunter! Here's no game for you except a tame doe that
belongs to me!"

After all the previously measured tempi, here is the first song marked simply "fast." The piano's texture is unlike anything heard up to this point: staccato-part writing, harsh with unloving, clashing sonorities. The prelude suggests the thrusting, invasive sound of the hunter's horn bursting into the miller's quiet world of flowing streams and predictable mill wheels. The singer is challenged by the tongue-twisting rapid-fire declamation, which in itself is an embodiment of torturous frustration. The miller is beside himself with jealous rage as everything he believes he has built is suddenly threatened. But just as importantly, the boy's vulnerability must be manifest. The previous songs suggest the miller has been waiting for disaster, but that does not take away his shock when it comes in the form of an assertive rival who surely spends no time gazing into mill brooks and imagining his own dissolution when he really should be making love. The shadows of the forest produce twin dangers, the hunter and the boar. Even before Darwin, those living close to nature understood the notion of the survival of the fittest. Like the happy trout of the famous song, the miller has enjoyed his time of sunlight, but now the other side of nature must work its irresistible will.

"Eifersucht und Stolz" (Jealousy and Pride)

> *"Where to so fast, dear brook? After our impudent hunter friend? Scold the mill girl for her loose, flirtatious ways. Go, brook, but don't tell her about my sadness. Tell her: 'He's cutting reed pipes to play pretty songs for children.'"*

The brook churns angrily in B minor to another "fast" tempo. The babbling brook has become something of a maelstrom, paralleling the boy's jealous rage. The very mention of the "Jäger" pulls the voice unpredictably upward. As if afraid of confronting the crisis at the source, he orders the stream back from visiting the hunter in short-breathed phrases, "Kehr' um," to confront the unfaithful girl for him instead. Verbally attacking her is evidently less frightening than confronting the being who threatens his existence so profoundly. To new melodic material, the miller asks the stream if it "saw" the girl "with craning neck, looking up the road." Her eager peering after her lover is set with unforgettable grotesquerie, the phrase "Mit langem Halse" drawn out from the top to the bottom of the singer's stave. The anger is palpable, almost violent. The rage is discharged further in a new musical phrase proclaiming in finger-wagging rhythmic curtness the "rules" that should govern "a nice girl" (sittsam Kind). The instrumental tags that punctuate the miller's rules about looking out windows recall nothing so much as sublimated hunting horns. The miller's personality clearly cannot withstand the threat of the hunter. Unnervingly, his own music seems all too ready to submerge itself into that of his enemy, just as the brook literally receives the miller in the last song. "Go tell her that, brooklet" (Geh', Bächlein, hin und sag' ihr das) is repeated in a rapid, scornful passage that quickly melts into a new, awkward vocal phrase, broken up as if the singer were overwhelmed by emotion.

"But don't tell her—[rest] do you hear, any word—[rest] about my sad expression." "Sad" (traurigen) is treated to a masochistically dragged-out phrase stretching over an entire musical bar. There is another pause, but now it represents the miller reflecting on the lie the brook should "tell" about him. "[Rest] Tell her—[rest]." And now the music for both voice and piano surges forward in a major key, momentarily buoyed by his fantasy: "He's with me cutting reed pipes" (Er schnitz bei mir sich eine Pfeif' aus Rohr). The miller's words and music attempt to recapture his lost contentment. The newfound sweetness of the vocal line would sound smug if not for the nervous, minor-key interjections of "Sag' ihr" (tell her), which interrupt the final page like an uncontrolled nervous tic, giving away the miller's game. He attempts cheerful nonchalance a final time with a luxuriant five-note decoration of the word "Lieder" as he imagines the cheerful songs he'll be performing for children. But the effect is exaggerated and undermined by the compulsive "Sag' ihr" iterations that bring this song of extraordinary psychological perception to its end.

"Die liebe Farbe" (The Beloved Color)

"I'll put on weeping-willow green, my girlfriend likes green so much. Dig me a grave and cover me with green grass, my girlfriend likes green so much."

Here the miller boy has his moment of tragic recognition, hinging on the true meaning of the fateful ribbon. The miller girl is in love, but not with him. The green ribbon he sent her as a love token that she now wears in her hair is, he now realizes, a symbol of the hunter, her true love. The musical pulse shifts to "somewhat slow" as the boy faces reality at last. The key of B minor is often associated with tormented eroticism in Schubert. The song expresses a static masochism. The pulsing staccato accompaniment suggests the sound of shell shock. "The game I hunt is death" (Das Wild, das ich jage, das ist der Tod) comes as an unwelcome surprise after the healthier anger of the preceding song. The repetitions (Mein Schatz hat's Grün so gern) ironically recall "Mit den grünen Lautenbande," but here the words and music drone fetishistically, almost insanely, as verse melts into verse. The keyboard writing for these droning words can suggest the sounds of distant hunting horns at the pianist's discretion. The miller boy's little world of the girl, the ribbon, the hunter, and the stream is slowly closing in on itself.

"Die böse Farbe" (The Hated Color)

> *"I'd like to go out and pull all the green leaves from every branch and make the green grass deathly white with my tears. Untie the green ribbon from your forehead, good-bye, good-bye! And give me your hand in parting!"*

This is a marvelous through-composed song expressing the quick fluctuations of the miller's emotional turmoil. The major key and ostensibly bolder pulse ("somewhat fast") contrast with the last song's numb grief. A new tone of defiance appears. Maybe this time at last the miller will find the means to survive. But this song's element of healthy self-assertion proves unsustainable. The miller's defiant posturing is colored by the passive optative, "I'd like" (Ich möchte). The keyboard prelude's first two bars, marked *piano*, present an oscillating, unstable motif, a picture of static frustration that is immediately discharged into a *forte* bar of angry chords. This is the very embodiment of passive-aggressiveness and the violently contrasting, ultimately impotent emotions about to be expressed.

The first vocal passage calls for ringing heroics from the singer as he asserts his desire to venture into the "wide world" (die weite Welt), a dramatic break from his narrow concerns. But this is instantly negated by the next phrase, "if only it weren't so green." Besides the words' neurotic content, the music here on "Wenn's nur so grün nicht wär'" contains a hint of the minor and the repetition of "so grün" recalls the last song's obsessiveness. Just as the miller hits this psychological impasse, the prelude's angry chords resound. More ringing would-be heroics follow on "I'd like to pluck (Pflücken) all the green leaves." The staccato chords in the piano writing under "Pflücken" picture the frantic plucking (Johnson 1989–97, 25: 52). Again the antiheroic music adorns the pathetic desire to whiten the grass with his tears. (Whiteness is now firmly a symbol of death, contrasting with the hunter's victorious, life-sustaining green.)

A recitative passage ensues wherein the miller interrogates the "hated color" (böse Farbe) directly, accusing it of "looking at [him] spitefully" (schadenfroh). The vocal line here slithers across the stave while the keyboard turns to soft staccato pulsations as the miller slides definitively into madness, the vocal line lurching haltingly, the keyboard rapidly. The words "proud" (stolz) and "arrogant" (keck) are set to ugly, dissonant little descending figures. The drawn-out vocal phrase "poor, pale man" (armen weissen Mann) is almost unbearable in its expression of vulnerability. The miller's barely coherent fantasy of camping out forever in stormy weather before the girl's door receives the heroic music we've heard before. But the hunter cannot stay out of his consciousness for long, and the piano erupts into a hunting horn pattern as he imagines his rival's call echoing through the forest. The miller's vocal line picks up the insistent, erotic energy as the miller imagines the sound luring the girl into his own line of sight. The miller asks the girl to remove his ribbon from her hair and, to the strains of the heroic music used so ironically before, to clasp his hand in a gesture of final farewell. The music swells to a genuine grandeur as the miller touches the girl for the first and last time of his life. But this moment of hard-won dignity is mercilessly undercut by the piano's repetition of the passive-aggressive prelude. The music creates the image of a life in the process of disintegration.

Act Five: Resignation and Death

"Trockne Blumen" (Withered Flowers) (CD Track 16)

> *"Bury me with all the now-faded flowers she gave me. Tears can't make dead love bloom again. Spring will come after winter and flowers will bloom, and when she walks by my grave she'll think, 'He was true-hearted.' Then bloom, you flowers; May is come and winter is over!"*

This is one of the summits of European music, yet takes less than four minutes to perform. The lied anticipates Debussy by nearly a century in its uncanny way of distilling natural sensory experience, as well as making audible the "spirit" of wilted flowers and the thawing of spring. (Debussy's piano prelude *Feuilles mortes* makes a fascinating comparison.) The slow, deadpan chords that open (0:00–0:07) and accompany the first half of the song are simple yet evocative: the sound of a faltering heartbeat, the essence of papery, crumbling roses. The vocal line hovering over the accompaniment like a garland of dead blossoms (0:08) is one of Schubert's most unforgettable. Two verses of this death music pass, and then Schubert effects one of his greatest miracles. The keyboard transitions from the minor to the major (1:53) and a curious figure emerges in the bass, a little tune of eight notes sounding first at the thought of the girl passing by his grave and her realization of the depth of his love. The eight-note tune begins an inexorable build, like the force of spring with all its regenerative powers rising from the bowels of the earth. (The nearest parallel for this passage is the hymn melody that arises in the middle of the the slow movement of the B-flat Sonata, D. 960.) The miller imagines all the dead flowers springing magically, triumphantly to life again. "May is come and winter is over!" (Der Mai ist kommen, / Der Winter ist aus; 2:17). The whole passage is repeated to an even more shattering climax (2:28–3:07), as if the miller is fetishistically replaying his suicide fantasy, imagining, as suicides often do, that he will somehow be there to appreciate her change of heart. But as the vocal line ends, the accompaniment grows softer (3:08) and begins an extended, darkening coda (3:14–3:29).

The eight-note spring tune sinks lower and lower on the keyboard like a fading chimera as the song ends. The miller's fantasy has, like all his other dreams, collapsed in upon itself.

"Der Müller und der Bach" (The Miller and the Brook)

The miller dialogues with the brook. He sings of his sorrow and the brook comforts him. The miller will seek "cool rest down below."

The miller's grief has brought him to the bank of his only "friend," the brook. As in some earlier songs, the psychic turbulence is refined into music of uncanny purity that could easily pass for folk song. The suicide's emotions are bound within the "innocent" formal restraint of the ABA structure. Again the sad heartbeat in the keyboard underlies a vocal garland in the minor key, but now the text is eerily impersonal— the miller is no longer fully a part of this world. His sad heartbeat and minor melody find a response in the brook's music of the next verse. The miller's G minor melody transforms into G major and the keyboard awakens the brook's characteristic rippling sounds. The tune of pain becomes a tune of consolation: a quintessential Schubertian paradox. The miller responds to his "friend" with his earlier G minor tune, but he is now supported not by his faltering heartbeat but by the brook's rippling patterns. By the simplest of means the miller becomes one with the brook. The final bars of solo accompaniment suggest his self-immersion in the water is a gentle, "natural" process.

"Des Baches Wiegenlied" (The Brook's Lullaby)

"Rock my boy to sleep. He will rest here till all awaken, sleeping away joy and sorrow. The moon rises. How vast heaven is!"

In this song, as in so much of Schubert's music, sentient and nonsentient nature meet in a loving communion that represents one of the composer's greatest gifts to humanity. This is a five-verse strophic song marked "moderate" to prevent interpreters from sentimentalizing it. The miller, as the brook says, has moved beyond joy and grief. The song's rhythm is frequently used in Schubert's music to depict the forces of nature at work. Even in death the hunter threatens the miller's peace, and the pianist may bring out the sublimation of the hunting horn buried within the keyboard writing during the relevant verse. Müller's words and Schubert's music allow us a glimpse of mysterious transcendence. A broken soul has found peace, the world expressed in the cycle has somehow healed itself, "and the heavens overhead stretch on and on" (Und der Himmel da oben, wie ist er so weit!).

Winterreise

chubert was keenly interested when he discovered yet another poetry cycle by Wilhelm Müller, whose *Die Schöne Müllerin* had served as the basis of his first great song cycle. He worked feverishly throughout 1827 on the new songs (D. 911). When asked by friends why he seemed so strangely reserved, he is supposed to have cryptically remarked, "Well, you will soon hear it and understand." Eventually he invited several close friends one evening to hear what he termed "a cycle of awe-inspiring songs." His friends were largely "dumbfounded by the gloomy mood," only "Der Lindenbaum" striking Schober as a lovely song (Deutsch 1958, 138). Mayrhofer was better able to grasp what his old friend had accomplished. Soon after Schubert's death he wrote: "He had been long and seriously ill, had gone through disheartening experiences, and life had for him shed its rosy color; winter had come for him. The poet's irony, rooted in despair, appealed to him; he expressed it in cutting tones. I was painfully moved" (15). Schubert's oldest friend, Spaun, recalled that the composer was disappointed by the general incomprehension and said, 'I like these songs more than all the others and you will get to like them too.' He was right, soon we were enthusiastic over the effect of these melancholy songs, which Vogl performed in a masterly way" (138). The twentieth-century composer Benjamin Britten, who frequently performed the cycle with Peter Pears, considered *Winterreise*, along with Bach's Mass in B Minor, to be one of the two pillars of Western music. Britten remarked: "Although he was only thirty [when Schubert wrote *Winterreise*] one feels it was [created] from the experience of a long lifetime." Pears added, "It's not a young man's music—it's sort of an ageless spirit's music. The whole of life is in it, like a psychiatrist's casebook; it has every situation in it of a distressed person" (BBC 1968).

Winterreise (Winter Journey) not only opens the door to a darker kind of romanticism, but also explores modes of expression that only the later impressionists, expressionists, and absurdists could match, but hardly improve upon. The unrelieved bleakness of the work is innovative not only for song and music in general but also in all the fine arts. One thinks of the psychological torment projected by the early twentieth-century expressionists, as well as Samuel Beckett's absurdist writing with its equally mysterious wanderers, hobos, and devastating bleakness. In other ways the unrelieved gray and white of *Winterreise* may find analogues in the paintings of Mark Rothko or the photo montages of Chuck Close, wherein repetition proves a potent entry point for exploring the self. Doubtless coming generations will discover other points of contact with this most searing and audacious of musical works. *Winterreise* contains many miracles. Perhaps the greatest is the fact that these songs, suffused with unrelenting despair, somehow move and exult an audience rather than depress it. The cycle is the greatest musical monument to humanity's ability to endure.

"Gute Nacht" (Good Night)

> *The wanderer introduces himself; he is departing from a community that had seemingly accepted him—"the girl spoke of love, her mother of marriage"—but now all is sadness and "the way lies in snow."*

We learn much about the wanderer, yet he remains a mystery. Like the human figures in Caspar David Friedrich's contemporary landscapes, we see his figure surrounded by a strangely numinous nature, yet never see his face. We never learn his name, his background, or why he is compelled to forsake all humanity. The opening modified strophic song serves as a musical portal of unexpected grandeur, akin in its own medium to the beginning chorus of Bach's *St. Matthew Passion*. The song's pulse indicates the wanderer's steady tread; the falling chromatic figure in the pianist's right hand is a gesture of grief that also recalls Bach for its restraint. One may also interpret the steady pulse of the accompaniment as the sensation of blood throbbing in the forehead, a symptom many feel with strong emotion such as unexpected, devastating rejection. The move toward the major on "The girl talked of love, her mother of marriage" (Das Mädchen sprach von Liebe, / Die Mutter gar von Eh') not only recalls happier times but also suggests something of the wanderer's quiet dignity; this is music of spiritual nobility as well as suffering. Nearly two bars of nagging, dissonant thirds send the tonality back to D minor as the protagonist returns to his present "sadness" (trübe) and the way that lies in snow (Der Weg gehüllt in Schnee). Just as King Lear in his madness rejects "all roofs to be comrade with the wolf and the owl," so Schubert's wanderer exiles himself to companionship with the moonbeams and the tracks of wild animals in the new-fallen snow.

The third verse offers slightly varied music. "Love loves to wander, —God made it that way—from one person to another" (Die Liebe liebt das Wandern,— / Gott hat sie so gemacht— / Von einem zu dem andern). These are some of the bitterest words in the cycle. The wanderer's relationship to God will figure again in "Mut." The last verse also has modified music for the closing lyrics as the wanderer seems to tiptoe past the sleeping beloved's door, leaving his note, "Good night," as a kind of macabre gift. The wanderer is not enraged; his music here is extraordinarily tender. He is a complex figure who responds to rejection and adversity with a unique combination of anger and compassion, resentment and love, madness and the ultimate sanity of consideration for others, even those who have hurt him the most grievously. Within the first song Müller and Schubert have created the one figure in the world of lieder who approximates the mystery and psychological depth of Shakespeare's Hamlet.

"Die Wetterfahne" (The Weather Vane)

"The weather vane on my beloved's house is as changeable as the people inside. She'll be a rich bride."

Here is the first example in *Winterreise* of proto-expressionistic elements. As with all expressionist art, we are compelled to see the world through the eyes of an anguished protagonist. Expressionism puts us inside the head of the artist-protagonist. Its hallmarks are distortion, a sense of terror, of a nightmare being enacted on the stage, on the canvas, or in the score. The chill wind is in the piano with all the darting uncertainty of the natural, unmediated world. The vocal line is violent and grotesque in its up-and-down motions, the musical equivalent of the distorted figures in paintings by Egon Schiele and Otto Dix ninety years later. Schubert ensures the singer will contrast his loud, hysterical proclamations with quieter observations; the wanderer's sanity becomes paradoxically more unstable the more gently he expresses himself in this nightmarish vision.

"Gefrorne Tränen" (Frozen Tears)

"My tears are frozen; I didn't know I was crying."

The image of the falling tears is uncannily evocative in the piano prelude. Gerald Moore observes, "No other song in the set seems to convey such an impression of biting cold, except the first part of "Auf dem Flusse." The flesh cringes and the blood congeals with these spiky detached chords in the pianoforte" (1975, 83). The song's middle section is some of Schubert's most frightening music. "Ah, my tears, are you so tepid you turn to ice?" (Ei Tränen, meine Tränen, / Und seid ihr gar so lau?). The voice lies low in the wanderer's register; the question directed at his own tears is dissonant, unsettling. The music shares something of the uncanny quality found in Boris Godunov's monologues in Mussorgsky's later opera. It is a musical rendering of a disturbed inner monologue. The wanderer wants to see his suffering as heroic. Surely his tears should be able to melt "all the winter's ice" (Des ganzes

Winters Eis), a grandiose thought that brings the song to its ringing, defiant conclusion.

"Erstarrung" (Numbness)

"I want to find where we walked; I'll burn through the snow with my hot tears."

This title is almost a misnomer considering the song's impression in performance. Schubert seems to have taken his cue from the reference to the wanderer "with [his] hot tears" (Mit meinen heissen Tränen). The image of a lava flow of tears burning through the ice animates the whole song. The wanderer desperately searches for places he has been with his beloved so as to carry some token away with him. He is terrified of forgetting her. The lurching, dissonant vocal line on "The flowers are withered, the grass looks so pale" (Die Blumen sind erstorben, / Der Rasen sieht so blass) signals psychological disturbance. But the composer also locates the universal with the particular. All people who have lost a loved one know this neurotic fear of forgetting their image or sound. Schubert's surging music captures this emotion perfectly.

"Der Lindenbaum" (The Linden Tree) (CD Track 17)

"There is the linden tree. I used to dream in its shade and carve loving words in its bark. I had to pass it at night. The rustling branches called to me, 'Come to me, friend, here you'll find rest!' The wind blew off my hat; I didn't return. Many hours have passed; I still hear the rustling."

This through-composed lied has become a folk song in German-speaking countries. No impressionist could better capture the movement of wind through the tree's branches than Schubert does in the opening for the piano (0:00–0:16). Just before the voice's entry the chords of contrasting *forte* and *più piano* (0:16–0:24) signal great spatial and temporal distance. The essence of the song is revealed before the wanderer begins singing. The spring winds that seem to rustle the tree's burgeoning branches are a figment of his memory. The main vocal melody recalls the beloved tree as an element of the wanderer's happier past. The shift to the minor (1:23) brings us closer to the present moment. "I must pass by it in the dead of night" (Ich musst' auch heute wandern / Vorbei in tiefer Nacht; 1:34). The sweetness of the major returns (2:13) as the tree "speaks" to him, "Come to me, friend, here you'll find rest!" (Komm her zu mir, Geselle, / Hier findest du deine Ruh'!). The sweetness is cloying and the promised "rest" is death, like the "games" promised by the Erlking ten years before. The branches offer a means to hang himself, but nature intervenes (2:30) with the wintery gusts that burst unpredictably from the keyboard, blowing off the wanderer's hat and sending the wretched man on his way. This is another instance in Schubert where the music partakes of natural phenomena in a way unrivaled except by Debussy. The meaning of the earlier contrast of *forte* and *piano* chords is clarified when they preface the final verse (2:57–3:07). "Now it's been many hours since I left that place" (Nun bin ich manche Stunde / Entfernt von jenem Ort). The gentle rustling of the branches returns as the postlude (4:16–4:34) after the wanderer ruminates that "there [he] would have found rest" (Du fändest Ruhe dort!). The lure of death will return in the cycle, but never with the seductive ambiguity found in this song.

"Wasserflut" (Flood)

> *"Many tears have fed the snow. When the snow melts the stream will bear it away. My tears in the water will burn when they flow by my love's house."*

This song's glacial pace presents one of the most mournful of melodies, with gestures in both the vocal line and accompaniment that vivify the words. Notice especially the setting of "[many tears] are fallen in the snow" (Ist gefallen in den Schnee). Comparison to Bach's vivid word painting is unavoidable. The rising cry on "[my] burning anguish" (das heisse Weh) is wrenchingly expressive.

"Auf dem Flusse" (On the River)

*"You used to murmur so happily; how still you are now, covered in
a crust of ice. My heart, don't you see your image in this brook?"*

The frozen river is unforgettably rendered with creepy staccato syncopa-
tions. The singer is asked repeatedly to sing "softly" as he contemplates
the icy current and slowly arrives at the song's moment of recognition,
that the frozen surface covering a raging torrent is an image of himself.
This discovery, a single verse that takes up half the song's length in its
elaborations, leads the singer to a shattering climax before the piano
resumes its macabre tune, seeming to wind out of earshot.

"Rückblick" (Looking Back)

*"The ground burns the soles of my feet; I can't stop running till I'm
away from the town. How different it was when I first came here
in springtime, you inconstant town! When I think of it I want to
run stumbling back to her door."*

The deeply agitated piano writing suggests the wanderer's stinging
humiliation as well as his frantic run as he tries to get out of town as
quickly as he can. The song's middle section transports us to the major
key and the wanderer's happy memories of his arrival—all was harmony and sweetness—all gone for good. The climbing vocal line on the
phrase "And ah, a girl's eyes glowed!" (Und ach, zwei Mädchenaugen
glühten!) begins to propel the song back to the present and the wanderer's mad run. But in the recapitulation of the opening music, the
thoughts of the girl begin to replace the humiliation. The notes on "I
want to stumble back again, to stand silently by her door" (ich zurücke
wieder wanken, / Vor ihrem Hause stille stehn) describe a grotesque
up-and-down pattern, suggesting the wanderer's anguished movements.
The pulse of the song slows as the wanderer makes his exhausted return
trip—at least in his imagination.

"Irrlicht" (Strange Impulse)

"A strange whim lured me into a chasm and I didn't even think about how I'd get out. I don't need directions; all suffering leads to the grave."

In Schubert's very personal key of B minor, the wanderer finds himself now free of the vestiges of civilization he had tried to flee in the last song. The key suggests the first decisive break from his fellow creatures. Only unfamiliar winter landscape surrounds him now. His only companion is the mysterious impulse or lure, the *Irrlicht* that seems to destabilize the piano's pulse with its contrary slow and staccato phrases, music that sounds like a sad, broken dance. The vocal line at points suggest the precarious physical position of the wanderer with its unpredictable motion. He no longer cares what lies ahead, and this signals a new phase of his tragedy.

"Rast" (Rest)

"I didn't know how tired I was till I lay down. I've found a place to sleep in an abandoned hut. But I can't sleep. The stillness brings up the pain."

The prelude suggests utter exhaustion and the wanderer's voice at first meshes perfectly with it. But he is not as numb as he would like to believe. The comment that "my back didn't feel the burden because the storm helped push me along" (Der Rücken fühlte keine Last, / Der Sturm half fort mich wehen) returns to extreme emotional turmoil with its angular, corrosive setting of the words. The effect is even greater when this same disturbing music is used for the song's closing lines, "[my heart,] you feel in the stillness the serpent biting with its bitter sting!" (Fühlst in der Still' erst deinen Wurm / Mit heissem Stich sich regen!). Music is here expressing the extremes of psychological torment. "Rest" seems hardly possible.

"Frühlingstraum" (Dream of Spring)

"I dreamed about flowers and springtime, but when the cock crowed it was dark and cold; the ravens screamed. But how did I see those flowers? Are you laughing at the dreamer? When will I hold my love in my arms?"

This song is constructed of three musical sections that are repeated to cover the poem's six stanzas. It is one of the greatest in the cycle, presenting an astonishing array of emotional extremes. Spring seems to have incongruously arrived with the lovely opening melody shared by piano and singer. Gerald Moore points out the cuckoo call implicit in the left hand's upward inflection just before the singer's entry (1999). This little detail, in the context of all the ice that surrounds the song, is almost over the top, a subtle hint that what is being portrayed is too good to be true. The second section, marked "fast," assaults the audience with its contrasting violence. All the "darkness and cold" (kalt und finster) is brought back with the line "ravens screamed from the hut's roof" (Es schrieen die Raben vom Dach), punctuated by rough chords on the piano. Now a "slow" section begins that, along with the secondary theme of the B-flat Sonata's opening movement and the Adagio of the String Quintet, may be the most immediately moving of all Schubert's melodies. "Who painted green leaves on the windows? Are you laughing at the dreamer who saw flowers in winter?" (Doch an den Fensterscheiben / Wer malte die Blätter da? / Ihr lacht wohl über den Träumer, / Der Blumen im Winter sah?). The wanderer's voice lowers on "Are you laughing at the dreamer?" creating the illusion that he is directly addressing the listener—one of the most intimate and heartbreaking moments in any lied.

The memory of the dream returns, made all the more poignant by the two sections that have gone before. It is the same music, but its effect is the more powerful for its familiarity and the even more emotive words garlanded by the sweet melody. The wanderer remembers "a beautiful girl," "cuddling and kissing," and "rapture and joy" (Von Wonne und Seligkeit), these last words treated to especially lovely decoration. Again the music is "fast," and violent agitation comes as he snaps out of his reverie to sit "alone" (alleine) and "think about the dream" (Und denke dem Traume nach). On the return of the almost unbearably beautiful third section, we learn that his allegedly frozen heart beats warmly when he merely closes his eyes. The man who seemed to have abandoned all hope and direction asks the now unanswerable question, "When will I hold my beloved in my arms again?" (Wann halt' ich mein Liebchen im Arm?).

"Einsamkeit" (Loneliness)

"I drift like a lonely cloud, all alone, no one to greet me."

The bitter key of B minor sounds again as the wanderer begins a slower, almost sleepwalking trudge (mit trägem Fuss) into the frozen world. The moments of illusory brightness in "Frühlingstraum" afforded just enough relief to make the lonely desolation of the present song the more striking. The melody of the first two verses partakes in that gypsylike mournfulness encountered throughout the cycle during passages in "Gefrorne Tränen," "Wasserflut," and "Rast." But just as a sense of numb desolation has been established, the wanderer and his music undergo the equivalent of a mental breakdown. The reality of the "calm air" and the "world's brightness," which counterpoint his agony, becomes too much to bear and a series of terrifying tremolos burst from the piano as the wanderer rails against the world and nature, which go about their business despite his pain. His loud outburst is followed by the muted trudging pattern in the piano as the wretched man moves on to the next station of his journey. This song prefigures the unexpectedly eruptive slow moments in Schubert's late instrumental works, such as the String Quintet and the A Major Piano Sonata, D. 959.

"Die Post" (The Mail Coach)

The horn on the mail coach has sounded. The excited wanderer has to remind himself it's not bringing any letter to him.

This song, like "Frühlingstraum," offers another striking contrast in mood. Set in E-flat major, a favorite key for wind instruments, the piano sounds out the merry tune of the post horn, which blew from mail coaches as they rode from town to town, announcing the mail's arrival. (In an earlier generation, Mozart featured just such an instrument in his "Posthorn" Serenade.) The pianist begins the steady rhythm of the horse hooves before sounding the horn's happy tune. The wanderer's vocal line, broken by expectant rests, suggests his (unrealistic) rising expectations. The horn's sound has taken him by surprise and brought him back to happier days. But reality inevitably breaks in during the minor-key section. He observes, "The post brings no letter for you" (Die Post bringt keinen Brief für dich), to music of restrained sadness. By the song's end, the wanderer ruefully admits he still cares about what happens back in his beloved's town.

"Der greise Kopf" (The Gray Head)

The wanderer wakes up with white hair that turns out, disappointingly, to be only snow. He wishes he were old and nearer to the grave.

It would be difficult to imagine a more fearless expression of despair or a greater contrast to "Die Post." Moore interprets the inspiration for the "long rising sweeps" in the music as stemming from the line "From dusk to morning light" (Vom Abendrot zum Morgenlicht). The gesture is "symptomatic of the constant anguish, [and] interminable nights our poor friend endures" (1975, 129). "The frost has strewn a white shine over my head." The dissonant, exotic vocal decoration of "strewn over my head" (Mir über's Haar gestreuet) is an uncanny, unsettling detail. Schubert is again exploring a new musical language for the expression of psychological disturbance. But even this passage pales besides the setting of the wanderer's ghastly exclamation, "How far off is the grave!" (Wie weit noch bis zur Bahre!), repeated with hollow, barren writing for voice and piano. Schubert was familiar with this feeling. He had written three years before to his friend Leopold Kupelwieser, "every

night when I go to sleep I hope never to wake again, and each morning
I am only recalled to the griefs of yesterday" (1970, 78).

"Die Krähe" (The Crow)

*A crow has been circling overhead. The wanderer addresses it in
friendly fashion. "Wonderful creature! At last I've found fidelity
till death."*

Here is the wanderer's first interaction with a living creature. The
piano's triplets capture the constant circling of the bird overhead. The
wanderer's voice moves in its own circular pattern as if hypnotized
by the bird's movements. He addresses the bird directly in one of the
cycle's most disconcerting passages: "Crow, wonderful creature, you
don't want to leave me? You're planning to feed on my body soon?"
(Krähe, wunderliches Tier, / Willst mich nicht verlassen? / Meinst
wohl bald als Beute hier / Meinen Leib zu fassen?). The singer has a
wide interpretive latitude here: irony, horror, indifference, or even
exhausted relief. The last lines are less ambiguous in their expression.
The voice and piano at first build a powerful crescendo full of anger and
irony on the injunction, "Crow, let me finally see fidelity that lasts to
the grave!" (Krähe, lass mich endlich sehn / Treue bis zum Grabe!). The
phrase is then repeated more gently, as a true prayer to the "wondrous
creature" that followed him from the "town of inconstancy."

"Letzte Hoffnung" (Last Hope)

*"I spot a single leaf left on the barren tree to pin my hopes on.
When the wind plays with it I tremble all over. If the leaf falls, so
do all my hopes."*

This is in some ways the most remarkable song of the cycle. The twentieth-century atonality of Schoenberg seems to have already arrived.
Tonality, rhythm, melody—all the familiar signposts for music making
in the 1820s seem shattered. The wanderer's skittish fantasies, his

ruined world could only be expressed this way. The song gains in terror when we realize the wanderer's world is really our world. All our hopes rest as inconstantly as his fragile single leaf awaiting the onslaught of that freezing wind. Musical "normality" is only reestablished as the wanderer lies on the ground "weeping on the grave of my hopes" (Wein' auf meiner Hoffnung Grab). The iterations and ornaments lavished on "wein'" partake of the gypsy, Eastern European sound that leaves so strong an imprint on these songs.

"Im Dorfe" (In the Town)

"The dogs bark; the people sleep, dreaming of good and bad. I'm beyond all dreaming; why stay here among the sleepers?"

This is almost as disturbing a song as "Letzte Hoffnung." The sense of tonality is secure, but what is the significance of the strangely threatening, lurching tremors and eery rests that serve as the song's prelude? We learn it is literally the barking of dogs straining against their chains, but it also "expresses a profound psychological disturbance" (Fischer-Dieskau 1978, 266). Presumably the wanderer is near a village, seeking a roof to sleep under, and this has alerted the watchdogs. The piano's rhythmic grinding is not loud; the wanderer is just on the outskirts of town, but the sound is enough to keep him away. The voice's melody follows its own dragging up-and-down trajectory, expressive of exhaustion and anxiety. He imagines the sleepers and their dreams that will "melt away when the morning comes" (Und morgen früh ist Alles zerflossen). Here Schubert creates a magical transition into a tender contrasting passage as the wanderer puts himself briefly in the position of the townspeople who still have something worth dreaming about. Another masterful transition brings back the wanderer's reality, the opening material, but this time his resentment begins to build against these lucky "sleepers." The anger is signaled by the repeated *crescendi* on "Why stay here among the sleepers?" (Was will ich unter den Schläfern säumen?). The unnerving "rattling" resumes as the wanderer leaves this last vestige of civilization.

"Der stürmische Morgen" (The Stormy Morning)

"The storm tears up the sky; lightning flashes. I see in this the likeness of my own heart."

The relatively slow tempi of the last three songs contrast with this short but vehement lied extolling a violent morning storm. "Der stürmische Morgen" injects a new energy into the cycle, carrying it to its conclusion. Cut off from normal human contact, the wanderer attempts to identify himself with the impersonal natural forces that surround him, not unlike Shakespeare's King Lear rushing into his storm, seeking to somehow join forces with it. Moore observes, "If 'Einsamkeit' expressed the fugitive's heaviness of spirit induced by calm bright weather, this stormy morning invigorates him and accords with his spleen" (1975, 147).

"Täuschung" (Delusion)

"A friendly light dances before me, luring me from my path. Maybe it's the way to a warm house? Delusion is all I have."

The contrast with the last song never fails to shock the listener. Heaven-rending chords are traded for innocuous, "rather fast" Biedermeier dance music, shared by voice and piano. It is the most sociable sound imaginable. For all his rage at rejection, the wanderer cannot live alone, and cannot part from the memory of "a bright warm house and a loving soul inside" (ein helles, warmes Haus, / Und eine liebe Seele drin). There is a passing hint at the minor key when he admits, "Ah, anyone as miserable as me gladly yields to such colorful illusion" (Ach, wer wie ich so elend ist, / Gibt gern sich hin der bunten List). The wanderer's self-knowledge allows the song to continue in its mirthless major key. "At the end of each line," Fischer-Dieskau notes, "the piano seems to parody the singer's words" (1978, 263).

"Der Wegweiser" (The Signpost)

"I have done no wrong to make me isolate myself and shun mankind. This signpost points in many directions. I'm on a road from which no one ever returns."

The rhythm of walking returns but the steady pulse is gone. The wanderer's theme again sounds a tone of eastern, Slavic desolation. He is struck by the injustice of his self-imposed isolation. The second verse transitions to the major with heartbreaking effect. "I haven't done anything to make me shun mankind" (Habe ja doch nichts begangen, / Dass ich Menschen sollte scheun). As with "Der greise Kopf," it is difficult not to think of Schubert's personal sufferings due to his illness helping to infuse these lines with such direct musical eloquence. Equally wrenching are the piercing high notes setting "[I wander] without rest and seeking rest" (Ohne Ruh', und suche Ruh'). Schubert's music italicizes these words, distilling the wanderer's present emotional state of near-spent exhaustion with great psychological insight. The last verse is the most important: "One signpost, unchanging, I see before me. One road I've got to travel from which no one ever comes back" (Einen Weiser seh' ich stehen / Unverrückt vor meinem Blick; / Eine Strasse muss ich gehen, / Die noch Keiner ging zurück). The wanderer's growing fixation on death is expressed by the hypnotically repeated notes that set these words and their repetition over two crescendoing passages in the piano, signaling his new determination. The expressive ornamentation given "Keiner" (no one) and the final, almost deadpan delivery of "die noch Keiner ging zurück" seem to bring the wretched man to the very edge of the grave.

"Das Wirtshaus" (The Inn)

The wanderer comes to a cemetery (the "inn"), but even death itself is closed to him.

It's hardly surprising the wanderer has brought himself to this most obvious of locations. What *is* surprising is that this is decidedly not the cycle's climax. The wanderer is rejected even from the land of the dead and is condemned, as it were, to live. All his experiences have led him to this pass, but Müller's text transcends easy cliché, contributing to the modernity of the poet's vision. The piano prelude and the vocal part sound a solemn, hymnlike melody, like the memory of an organist playing at a funeral. The tune's sweet sadness and the slow pulse contribute to a sense of unreality that hovers over this and the penultimate song, "Die Nebensonnen." It is increasingly difficult to tell what is "real" in the wanderer's experiences and what imagined. What is unchallenged, however, is his dogged resolution at the song's close. With even the "inn" closed to him, he steels himself to soldier on. The final words resonate with some of the cycle's noblest music, the epitome of Schubert's singular brand of quiet heroism. "On then, ever onward, my trusty walking staff!" (Nun weiter denn, nur weiter, / Mein treuer Wanderstab!). The *Wanderstab* is a kind of hiking staff still used today in central Europe, but is particularly evocative of romantic wanderers. The definitive visual image appears in Caspar David Friedrich's famous painting *The Wanderer and the Sea of Clouds*.

"Mut" (Courage)

> *"When my heart complains, I sing. I don't listen to it. If there's no God on earth, then we are gods ourselves!"*

In Müller's original poetic order, this was the next-to-the-last song. Schubert moved it forward to avoid placing two hymnlike songs together ("Das Wirtshaus" and "Die Nebensonnen") as well as to lend more weight to "Die Nebensonnen." "Mut" is the last of the "walking" songs and also the most vigorous. The wanderer's bravado sounds painfully hollow as he brags of ignoring the winter's affronts to his senses and the "speech" (spricht) of his heart. The last two lines are repeated with an almost demented gusto: "If there's no God on earth, then we are gods ourselves" (Will kein Gott auf Erden sein, / Sind wir selber Götter). Amazingly, Metternich's censors ignored such proto-Nietzschean heresy.

"Die Nebensonnen" (The Phantom Suns)

> *"I saw three suns in the sky. You are not my suns. My best two suns have set; if only the third would follow, I'd rather be in the dark."*

This is easily the most mysterious song Schubert ever composed. Scholars have argued for years about the meaning of Müller's ambiguous lines: are the suns mere hallucinations, some kind of religious symbolism, or the real sun and the two eyes of the girl who is lost forever? The only imperative is that the answer to the song's riddle be one that the performers can invest with all of their expressive strength, for Schubert's setting is of the profoundest feeling. The hymnlike melody in A minor, one of the composer's most tragic keys (he wrote three dark piano sonatas in this key alone), betokens unbearable loss. Perhaps the wanderer has entered a mental realm where clear communication, even to the most sympathetic listeners, is increasingly impossible. This is a kind of interiority new in Western music. One thinks of the Shakespearean critic Samuel Johnson's observation that Hamlet's "To be or not to be" soliloquy seems only partly comprehensible, as if real thought were rendered aloud.

"Der Leiermann" (The Hurdy-Gurdy Man) (CD Track 18)

> *The wanderer meets a barefoot hurdy-gurdy player, alone and evidently insane. He asks him, "Will you sound your music to my songs?"*

For the first and only time in the cycle, the wanderer confronts another human being. The hurdy-gurdy was an instrument favored by beggars during Schubert's time. It can be carried much like an accordion. A small keyboard is played by one hand while the player's other hand maintains the instrument's sound, a squally, nasal drone, by continuously operating a hand crank. The piano creates that drone, a sad, broken little tune (0:00–0:30) that turns in upon itself, like the proverbial broken record. Significantly, the hurdy-gurdy man is an artist of sorts who stands "beyond the village" (hinter'm Dorfe; 0:30), turning the crank of his pathetic instrument without a single coin. "Barefoot on the ice, he staggers here and there" (Barfuss auf dem Eise / Wankt er hin und her; 1:01), his collection plate forever empty. Accompanied only by "snarling dogs" (Hunde knurren; 2:15) his loneliness mirrors that of the wanderer. The poor man has no audience, no hope, and yet he carries on, grinding out his repetitive tune for a hostile universe. Like the wanderer, he is alone, seeming to let things "come as they may" (wie es will; 2:34). Here is one of those many moments in Schubert where attempting to define him as a romantic or a classicist becomes absurd. The meeting of these two wretched hobos carries the sublimity of mad Lear and blind Gloucester's encounter at Dover or perhaps even more accurately, the postapocalyptic world of Beckett in the mid-twentieth century.

The final verse is the most uncanny. The wanderer addresses a fellow man for the first time (3:29) in a disarmingly conversational, *parlando* style. "Wonderful old fellow, shall I go with you? Will you turn your hurdy-gurdy to my songs?" (Wunderlicher Alter, / Soll ich mit dir gehn? / Willst zu meinen Liedern / Deine Leier drehn?). We may recall the similarly eery address to the crow, "Wunderliches Tier," in "Die Krähe." Graham Johnson observes: "As if in an attempt to give a sample of his wares, the singer leaves the reaches of speech, and suddenly sings his heart out with leaps of an octave . . . a mournfully elongated E-natural on '*drehn*' for three beats [3:50–3:54]. . . . Thus a powerful streak of color suddenly appears, comet-like, in the blank winter sky, and just as quickly disappears" (1989–97, 30: 105).

Some commentators suggest that the "Leiermann" is a symbol of death itself, like the maniacal violinist who invades the scherzo of Mahler's Fourth Symphony. This is certainly possible, but a more literal interpretation yields even more powerful resonances. The organ grinder is a doppelgänger for both the wanderer and the composer himself. As a syphilitic, Schubert would have been aware of what potentially lay ahead for him in the final stages of the disease. Syphilitic dementia can manifest itself as endlessly repetitive behavior, rendered musically as the constant droning of the hurdy-gurdy. The modern equivalent of the hurdy-gurdy man can be seen easily in a modern big city; one thinks of the pathetic, often half-mad buskers who frequent the New York subway system. Schubert is confronting his greatest fear directly and rendering it into art. The composition of this song must have been an act of almost unimaginable courage and, one hopes, of an equally compensatory catharsis.

Schwanengesang

chwanengesang (Swan Song), D. 957, comprises the last songs Schubert composed before his unexpected decline and death in November 1828. They were issued the following year under the sentimental title given them by their publisher, Tobias Haslinger, who was eager to cash in on the postmortem surge of interest in the composer. *Schwanengesang* represents a seemingly accidental gathering of two distinct groups of songs by two poets who were new or relatively new to Schubert—Rellstab and Heine—as well as a single setting of a piece by Schubert's friend Seidl.

On one level, *Schwanengesang*'s desperate parts attest to a life interrupted, the young man's equivalent to old Bach's unfinished Contrapunctus in *The Art of Fugue*: yet another manifestation of the fragility of human aspiration. Yet *Schwanengesang* holds together as powerfully as the two Müller cycles. The three poets were close to Schubert in age. All of the cycle's songs are united by the theme of longing (Sehnsucht), the quintessential romantic emotion, creating a musical mosaic that contains greater extremes than either of the earlier cycles. *Schwanengesang* opens and closes with songs about go-betweens in love affairs: the rushing brook of "Liebesbotchaft" and the carrier pigeon of "Die Taubenpost." As superb as each song is on its own, the *Schwanengesang* lieder gain enormously when they are performed together. Rather than revealing differing aspects of a single protagonist as the performer of the earlier cycles must do, the singer of *Schwanengesang* must be a quick-change artist, moving from one persona to another. Yet the overall effect of the cycle is one of cohesion. Could the idea of grouping these last sets together have been Schubert's after all, conceived during his final illness and passed on to his brother Ferdinand, in whose house the composer died?

Here is Schubert consolidating all he has learned about song composition and life itself while breaking into terrifying new emotional territory in the six Heine songs, arguably the high-water mark of all European, let alone German art song, just before his voice is silenced. (Indeed, the Heine set was not equaled in its searing intensity until the music of Mahler and Berg.) Like the sketches of his recently discovered Tenth Symphony, D. 936a, *Schwanengesang* reminds us that Schubert's death a few weeks short of his thirty-second birthday represents perhaps the most obscene loss in the history of art.

The Rellstab Group

Shortly before his death, Beethoven had been considering collaborating with the Berlin poet and music critic Ludwig Rellstab (1799–1860) on an opera. Rellstab had given some of his poems to Beethoven either to set as songs or as examples of his ability. On his deathbed in March 1827, the older composer is said to have examined some of Schubert's songs and been profoundly affected, exclaiming, "Truly, this Schubert has the divine spark!" This incident inspired Beethoven's friend and assistant Anton Schindler to pass some Rellstab poems on to Schubert later that year. The care that Schubert lavished on these implies how seriously he took the gift, a symbolic inheritance from the revered dead master. "Auf dem Strom" (On the River), D. 943, is discussed in Chapter 7. Another seven poems were set sometime between Schindler's delivery of the texts and August 1828, the date on the manuscript.

"Liebesbotschaft" (Love's Message)

> *"Rushing brooklet, are you going by my beloved's house? Carry her my greetings. Whisper to her dreams of love."*

"The soul of man is like the water; it comes from heaven, it rises to heaven, and down again to earth it must come, ever changing. . . .

Soul of mankind, how like the water! Fate of mankind, how like the wind!" These words from Goethe's poem "Gesang der Geister über den Wassern" (Song of the Spirits Over the Waters) held such fascination for Schubert that he set them repeatedly in various vocal and instrumental combinations over the course of several years. The lines are important for understanding something of the composer's essential nature, as well as the surprising depths to be found in the present song's "little stream." Much of Schubert's music flows with the rhythm of natural phenomena, such as water, breezes, winds, or heartbeats. Schubert captures better than any composer save perhaps Debussy the unpredictability of the natural world, its eternal processes, its eternal state of becoming, its blessedness, and its threatening aspects. Maybe this is why Artur Schnabel called Schubert the composer "closest to God."

One of Schubert's last water songs is also one of his most characteristic and bewitching creations. When the "somewhat slow" tempo indication is observed, the keyboard writing is allowed to flow and gurgle gently like lapping wavelets tinged in a G major glow, akin to the flowing "waters" of the G-flat Impromptu, D. 899, no. 3. The "silvery and bright stream" of "Liebesbotschaft" exists in an idealized Biedermeier landscape but partakes of something higher. It is both a metaphor of beautiful, ever-changing nature and a symbol of the composer's powers of self-renewing creativity. The *Bächlein* is the medium of the lover's communication and the vehicle that conveys the listener into the rarefied world of Schubert's last songs.

The song is through-composed. The main theme of the first verse is as sunny as the gently lapping accompaniment. But this major-key sunshine easily darts into the minor, reminding us of the presence of potential sorrow even in this most ostensibly cheerful of songs. Particularly notable is the way the keyboard's "water" reflects and comments soloistically after each verse—a musical equivalent of water's reaction to human movement. The third verse is set to slower, minor-tinged music in the vocal line, perfectly reflective of the girl dreaming beside the stream. The singer seems lost in the drowsy sensuality of this image, only to abruptly shake it off with more vigorous music on "comfort the sweet one with your friendly gaze, for her beloved will soon return" (Tröste die Süsse / Mit freundlichem Blick, / Denn der

Geliebte / Kehrt bald zurück). This phrase is immediately repeated, building a surprising sense of urgency and leading to nearly four bars of transitional material for the pianist that is among the most sublime in the instrument's literature. Simply put, the minor-keyed water music shifts to the major for a recapitulation of the song's opening. A seemingly routine operation, but Schubert is arguably at his most inspired in the startling ways he modulates from key to key, making us hear the familiar in unexpected ways that alter our perception of the world, as all great art does. The piano's bass, not for the first or even last time in Schubert, gives through the simplest of patterns a brief but spine-tingling intimation of something uncanny, the spirit of water, if you will, or a sense of God "moving on the face of the waters," lifting Rellstab's poetry to realms of feeling that lie beyond words.

The opening music now serves the singer's images of the setting sun and his desire for the brook to "cradle [his] beloved in slumber" (Wiege das Liebchen / In Schlummer ein) while "whispering dreams of [his] love to her" (Flüstre ihr Träume / Der Liebe zu). This last idea is repeated to languorous, ever-softening music. The key word "Liebe" is accented by a five-note setting drawn out over two bars. The beloved is put tenderly to sleep in the singer's imagination and with the help of the babbling brook's gentle postlude.

"Kriegers Ahnung" (Soldier's Foreboding)

> *"My brother soldiers are sleeping around me, but I'm restless and full of longing. How often I've slept on her sweet breast before the fire. But take comfort, heart; there are battles to come. Soon I will rest and sleep well. My darling, good night!"*

This is the least loved song of the cycle, virtually never performed outside the complete set. As a portrait of "burning longing" (Sehnsucht... so heiss), no song more deserves its place in *Schwanengesang*. The choice of text and its handling reveals how far Schubert had matured from his simplistic visions of warfare in his early songs. The threat of Napoleon led to several warrior songs in the 1810s marked by unreflective jingoism. "Kriegers Ahnung" presents a real, not a chocolate or tin soldier, his outer and inner worlds vividly presented as in an operatic scene. This warrior wrestles with the threat of his own extinction and expresses frankly his longing for love, sex, and comfort before the looming morning's battle. In this sense, his situation is similar to Cavaradossi's in his aria before his execution in Puccini's *Tosca*. Schubert's soldier, however, becomes almost emotionally incoherent at the thought of leaving life, before a cold irony and bitterness set in, demonstrating how little the twenty-first century could have taught the mature Schubert about supposedly modern psychology. This "Krieger" is the direct forerunner of all Mahler's songs of hapless soldiers, just as *Winterreise*'s hero is father to Mahler's wayfarer some sixty years later.

The keyboard prelude begins with hushed drumbeats, anticipating many a Mahlerian march. The protagonist sings of the "circle of my brothers-in-arms . . . [who] lie around me in deep sleep" (In tiefer Ruh liegt um mich her / Der Waffenbrüder Kreis). The terse strictness of the beat and minor tonality set the scene. "My heart is so apprehensive and heavy" (so bang und schwer) is set to a menacing melodic turn, as rigid as the keyboard's drumbeats. But the "hot longing" sends the voice into higher territory, the soldier's desire leading to an attractively curved ornament on "so heiss," a thought also immediately repeated with a downward-swooping decoration on "Sehnsucht." The drumbeats return, only to fade gently into silence. We are leaving the soldier's material surroundings and entering the world of his memories. New music with even-flowing triplets, a "gemütlich" oasis, takes over as the soldier recalls "dreaming sweetly on her warm breast" (süss geträumt / An ihrem Busen warm!) and the "friendly glow of the hearth fire" (freundlich schien des Herdes Glut) as "she lay in my arms" (Lag sie in meinem Arm!). The memory of the "warm breast" and "in my arms" are savored in repeats, each to be sung more gently than before, as if each time the soldier recalls his distance from that scene. The triplets spin on their own for over a measure before the bottom falls out of the revelry with a move to a newly militant, stressful pulse. The singer's remembered hearth fire is replaced by the "dark flames" of the campfire "playing off of the weapons" before him (Hier, wo der Flammen düstrer Schein / Ach! nur auf Waffen spielt) as the voice sings a new, more urgent minor-key melody. The C-sharp on "ach" seems to capture the moment he discerns the weapons in the flickering light. "Here the breast feels completely alone" (Hier fühlt die Brust sich ganz allein), a sentiment made unforgettably palpable by the singer's climbing vocal register. The soldier has come to the breaking point.

New music of scarcely contained anxiety emerges from the keyboard. The soldier repeats, "Heart, don't lose comfort!" (Herz! Dass der Trost dich nicht verlässt!) to a nervously climbing figure in crescendo, the words contradicting the increasing turbulence of his music. The reason for "comfort" is "Many battles are yet to come" (Es ruft noch manche Schlacht). "Battles" (Schlacht) is drawn out disturbingly on a loud, sustained E for over a bar. The soldier's panicked realization that he is trapped in ongoing warfare soon shifts back to softer, more "gemütlich" sentiment on "Soon I'll rest well and sleep sound, dearest love—good night!" (Bald ruh' ich wohl und schlafe fest, / Herzeliebste—Gute Nacht!). The transitions between threatening and consoling music, the dynamic extremes and the emotional shifts they project perfectly portray a soul trapped in a moment of reckoning in which he has lost all control over his fate. The "gemütlich" sweetness is short-lived as the sung melody and its accompaniment transition unexpectedly back to the song's opening. The soldier sadly intones "Herzliebste—Gute Nacht!" without sweet nostalgia or biting irony. Only a grim awareness of his inescapable surroundings can be heard in his slow, death-march rhythm while the keyboard returns to its drumbeat pattern. The song has an extraordinary musical-dramatic architecture that becomes apparent once we recognize the wide territory of past and present, inner and outer worlds that it has spanned only to return us, unexpectedly, to the musical point of departure.

"Frühlingssehnsucht" (Spring Longing)

> *"The sensual delights of springtime fill the air, luring me onward, but to where? Only you can liberate these forces in me!"*

The death anticipated in "Kriegers Ahnung" is contrasted with the personification of the life force in this, Schubert's last spring song. "Frühlingssehnsucht" is a modified strophic lied. Many performers allow it to drag, failing to observe Schubert's explicit marking of "fast," demanding a sustained burst of energy contrasting with both of the earlier songs. The piano prelude flows like a gust of warm spring air, setting the atmosphere of joyous suspense and sensual excitement. The first four verses are given music that suggests breathless anticipation. Singer and keyboard seem to surge toward a kind of musical/sexual climax near the end of each verse when the poet recognizes his own emotional involvement with the nature surrounding him. This building exultation is always blocked by a haunting minor-key barrier on the questioning refrains "Where to?" (Wohin?), etc. But the poet's self-interrogation leads to a final verse set in a minor-keyed variant of the main tune: "Restless longing! Yearning heart!" (Rastloses Sehnen! / Wünschendes Herz!). As the human subject joins the blooming world, Schubert varies the song's theme with all of his customary sensitivity to emotional ambivalence. The singer finds his rather explicit release with the iterated "you" (du) sung to the highest note in the song. "Du" is repeated twice to forceful chords before the keyboard postlude trails away in rapid decrescendo, all passion spent, all ambiguity resolved in the arms of the lover.

"Ständchen" (Serenade) (CD Track 19)

"Softly my songs plead to you in the night. The nightingales join me in singing. They know the pain of love. Don't fear any betrayers. Come to me, love. Why do you delay? Come, make me happy!"

The unforgettable melody and the keyboard's charming imitation of the serenader's guitar have made this one of the most beloved and popular songs ever written. Its D minor tonality, shared with the most harrowing of Schubert's string quartets, "Death and the Maiden," D. 810, and the song's portrayal of "Sehnsucht" in its most anguished guise should alert the listener that this is more than just another pretty love song. This courting song written by an ailing syphilitic is really a dark and ghostly work. For all its obvious passion, the melody bears such a strong sense of melancholy that it is hard to imagine this most famous of sexual entreaties being positively answered.

The pianist's music (0:00–0:09) plucks out the guitar tune. In a sensitive performance, the left-hand bass chords add just enough indication of anxiety that the music avoids any hint of quaintness. The dark main vocal melody and Rellstab's words fit as perfectly as any music and text have ever conjoined. "My songs gently float toward you through the night" (Leise flehen meine Lieder / Durch die Nacht zu dir). The piano, in its role as guitar, strums exquisite echo passages after each verse (0:20–0:24, 0:35–0:39). The words, melody, and accompaniment conjure the scene before the listener with all the musical-dramatic economy found in a Mozart opera or for that matter a Shakespearean play, wherein poetry and gesture allowed a noonday audience at the Globe Theater to "see" the nocturnal scenes that open *Hamlet* or *Macbeth.* "The slender treetops whisper as they rustle in the moonlight" (Flüsternd schlanke Wipfel rauschen / In des Mondes Licht; 0:40). A good Schubert singer will use these wonderful words and the music that sets them to further create the scene, allowing listeners to somehow see the treetops in the color of the voice and the marvelous sounds of the words. The ornament on "in des" (0:45) is one of the song's most endearing details, giving pleasure whenever it is repeated throughout the work. It sounds like a wisp of some long-lost courtly elegance.

The silver-toned nightingales in the second verse (1:34) are hugely romantic images to audiences of Schubert's time and our own. But an educated listener of early nineteenth-century Europe would have recalled the darker mythic background of these birds. The ancient Greeks associated the nightingale's song with a ghastly love triangle involving rape, mutilation, and cannibalism. The birds are the transformed victims and perpetrators of this horror, sublimating their agony in exquisite song throughout eternity. They do indeed "understand the bosom's desire, they know the pain of love" (Sie verstehn des Busens Sehnen, / Kennen Liebesschmerz; 2:04). This recollection informs both the text and the music and gives context to the almost frightening new music given the last verse.

The *forte* marking at the end of the first two stanzas (2:38) hints at the protagonist's slowly building passion and anxiety. Who are these "betrayers" (Verräters) whom the mysterious "Liebchen" fears? The protagonist loses composure as he doubts that the beloved will come.

"Trembling, I await your arrival!" (Bebend har' ich dir entgegen!) is delivered with a searing intensity (2:47), almost rupturing the song's decorum, the keyboard's echo including a similarly impassioned refrain. The protagonist still has the artistic control to make his strumming follow his singing. The courtly ornaments return beguilingly (2:56–3:08) on the iterated "Come, make me happy!" (Komm', beglücke mich!). But on the final repeat of "beglücke mich!" (3:09–3:18) the flourish is gone, the music is growing softer, and the voice is sinking lower on the stave, as if slowly drooping back to the song's starting point; the smoldering passion seems spent, indicated further by the keyboard's bars of solo strumming (3:19–3:39), which grow ever fainter till the end. Hardly an image of successful seduction, "Ständchen" seems more a kind of musical coitus interruptus, a fragment of consciousness that seems to endlessly rerun in the protagonist's mind. Did the girl ever come? Did she even exist? Surely the "old love sorrows" the protagonist of "Der Doppelgänger" recalls must have sounded something like this.

"Aufenthalt" (Refuge)

> "Rushing stream, raging forest, jutting rock; my refuge. My pain endures like primal ore in stone."

Antigone, Sophocles's tragic heroine, en route to her rocky tomb, compares herself to Niobe, the mother whose children were murdered by the gods and whose grief was so profound that she was transformed into an ever-weeping stone. "The saddest of deaths . . . turned to stone . . . the rains never leave her, nor the snows" (*Antigone* ll. 885–88). A similar fate threatens the protagonist of "Aufenthalt." "My pain endures like primal ore in stone" (Und wie des Felsen / Uraltes Erz, / Ewig derselbe / Bleibet mein Schmerz). The wanderer's anguish drives him into a natural world that absorbs him: the raging river, the angry forest, tormented trees, and sharp, jutting stone. One of the more retrospective songs in the cycle, "Aufenthalt" recalls the idea of the storm within explored by the protagonist in "Die junge Nonne," D. 828, as well as the numinous nighttime forest of "Im Wald," D. 708. At the same time, the piece's exploration of solitary angst and occasionally flinty-sounding accompaniment serves as a harbinger of "Der Atlas."

The peculiar beauty of "Aufenthalt" emerges when, instead of the choppy, "little engine that could" tempo to which pianists often subject the opening prelude, the song is allowed to open and flow as Schubert directed, "Not too fast, but with strength." "Not too fast" permits the fateful pulsations that drive the work to make their impact without preventing the gorgeous, cellolike melody from sounding in the keyboard's bass. The song's five verses are set to a ABCBA pattern. The first affords the singer a rich, grumbling minor-keyed theme combining feelings of anger and grief, which epitomize romantic suffering: "Raging river, roaring forest, jutting rock, my refuge" (Rauschender Strom, / Brausender Wald, / Starrender Fels / Mein Aufenthalt). The second verse is set to a variant of this theme, which rises in an appropriately seething vocal line like the "wave after wave" (Wie sich die Welle / An Welle reiht) image in the text until the protagonist reaches the first of the songs' stabbing climaxes on "Tränen," "[his] ever-renewed tears" (Tränen / Mir ewig erneut).

The third verse is treated magically: the keyboard seems to brighten into the major as the image of "high treetops surging" (Hoch in den Kronen / Wogend sich's regt) sends the vocal line into its higher reaches while the pianist's one hand plays a cellolike doubling of the singer's line, the other hand continuing the anxious chord patterns. The thought of the high air makes the wanderer forget his plight. This moment of unexpected relief is exquisite, though momentary. "In Schubert, the major key is the dream, the minor is reality," as Alfred Brendel has often remarked. The wanderer's "endlessly pounding heart" (unaufhörlich . . . Herze schlägt) draws his music back down. The seething variant of the leading motif returns, music befitting the "primal ore" and abiding grief. Another keyboard interlude leads to the return of the first verse and its vocal melody, so redolent of the quintessential, rebellious outsider. The stunning *fortissimo* on "Fels," the jutting "rock," which the singer holds for almost three anguished bars, marks a final cry of despair. The voice is silent while the sounds of an internalized, inhospitable nature rumble on, the cello theme moaning softly in the bass as the song dies.

"In der Ferne" (In the Distance)

"Woe to the fugitive who abandons the world, forgetting his home. Murmuring breezes and curving waves, send my greetings to the one who broke my heart!"

As impressive as the Heine settings, "In der Ferne" is an unfairly neglected song. It serves as the emotional anchor for the Rellstab songs just as "Der Doppelgänger" does for the Heine group. It seems no accident that both of these poetic texts deal with the extreme alienation felt when love is betrayed, and both songs are in B minor. "In der Ferne" traces an emotional journey not unlike that of *Winterreise*, and its protagonist shares something of that earlier wanderer's tragic grandeur.

The piano prelude creates a broken, strangely lurching pattern, exploring in only a few measures extremes of volume and chordal texture. A mysterious motif climbs tentatively from the bass, like a futile search for light. Emotional shock and reaction, as well as intimations of nearness and distance, are already manifest before the voice enters with a melody almost entirely locked onto a dour F-sharp. "Woe to the fugitive, who abandons the world" (Wehe dem Fliehenden / Welt hinaus ziehenden!). A measure of solo keyboard ensues, creating in a single bar a ghostly echo effect, spatial and emotional emptiness rendered into sound. The singer continues his slow, dirgelike melody. His voice climbs upward as his pain intensifies on "hating his mother's house, abandoning his friends, without any blessing to send him on his way!" (Mutterhaus hassenden, / Freunde verlassenden / Folget kein Segen, ach! / Auf ihren Wegen nach!). This last thought, of an unblessed journey, is immediately reiterated with the voice being pulled downward by grief. In a world before quick or relatively safe transportation, leave-taking from family or friends took on a more hallowed significance than we may imagine. The long, dragging emphasis on "Wegen nach!" challenges the singer's breath and pitch control. In performance one can sometimes detect the strain, and this is not necessarily a bad thing. Schubert has created a physical difficulty for the singer that directly conveys the protagonist's anguish. The keyboard prelude is repeated, gaining in significance from what has gone before.

The second verse offers the first vocal melody with several piquant variants and greater contrast between dynamic extremes. The evening star "sinking hopelessly" (Hoffnungslos sinkender!) drags the voice down again to languishing low notes. The musical depiction is, if anything, even more vivid here than at "Wegen nach!" and this second test of the singer's control of pitch and breath brings the protagonist to his lowest emotional state. The music is almost literally torturous, like the alienation expressed in the poem. Again the keyboard prelude's lurching refrain sounds, marking the nadir of the singer's self-laceration.

The final verse initiates another of the song's many surprises. "Murmuring breezes, waves gently curling, sunbeams quickening, lingering nowhere, send greetings to the one who broke my faithful heart with pain, greetings from the fugitive, the one who flees out into the world." A major-keyed variant begins in the vocal line, creating the effect, as so often in Schubert, of sunlight piercing through clouds. The keyboard, taking its cue from the mention of breezes, articulates a rustling pattern. Private human suffering having reached its limit, the protagonist at last admits the outside world into his consciousness, breaking his emotional impasse. The rhythms of the natural world take over the song, seeming at first to heal the wanderer, as reflected by the radiance of his vocal line. But bitterness is never far away. On mention of "pain" (Schmerze, ach!) and "heartbreak" (Herze brach) the melody slips into the minor and the vocal line drops out, allowing the keyboard a bar of echo effect as in the earlier verses. Now, however, the music is so full of motion that the appalling emptiness is gone, replaced by a pulsating emotion, suffused with anger but also suggesting that the wanderer's will to live, his mysterious kinship with the natural world, will sustain him even in his present extremes. Schubert offers a generous elaboration of the final verse, the music's beauty helping the protagonist to transcend the purely spiteful sentiments that Rellstab's text by itself offers the reader. The opening idea of nearness and distance returns. "Welt hinaus ziehenden!" (The one who flees out into the world) is given special emphasis with long-breathed elaborations on "ziehenden," testing the singer's control one final time in a higher vocal register as the keyboard grows softer, as if traveling across the void to the unfaithful one.

"Abschied" (Good-bye)

"Good-bye, you happy little town! My horse is ready. You've never seen me sad before and you won't now. Good-bye, little twinkling window. You're so inviting. Good-bye, stars; you can't compete with that little window. I don't need your light. Good-bye!"

The final Rellstab song is one of the most beloved. Dietrich Fischer-Dieskau ended many of his Schubert recitals with it after giving plentiful encores, often getting a chuckle from the audience as he sang about his need to leave "[this] lively, happy city" (Du muntre, du fröhliche Stadt). As a song of farewell, it was a perfect cap to Schubert's Rellstab group, and he took pains to contrast its seemingly cheerful mood with the overtly anguished soul-searching that has gone before. Like "Ständchen," it is a song about singing, as the protagonist implies that the entire lied is an "Abschiedsgesang." "Abschied," however, would not be a Schubert song if it did not contain its share of emotional ambiguities and mysteries. Why must the protagonist "leave [this] lively city"? Who lives or lived in the cottage? How much of the singer's outward cheerfulness is forced? The closing lines, as we will see, are particularly ambiguous.

"Abschied" is a loose-limbed through-composed song that disguises itself as a strophic one. The music for each verse is slightly varied to match the poetry. All of its verses begin and end with the declaration "Good-bye!" (Ade!). The rider first addresses the "lively, happy city." His reference to his horse's eager pawing of the ground (Schon scharret mein Rösslein mit lustigem Fuss) inspires the joyous staccato hoofbeats that animate the keyboard writing. The town "has never seen me unhappy and isn't about to now at parting" (Du hast mich wohl niemals noch traurig gesehn, / So kann es auch jetzt nicht beim Abschied geschehn). The jaunty vocal line and happily trotting keyboard repress whatever latent regret lies within these words. The "trees," "gardens," and "stream" have only heard happy songs from him before, so his "farewell song sounding far and wide" (Weit schallend ertönet mein Abschiedsgesang) will be no different. Some "friendly girls" flirt with him; he looks them over, but refuses to "turn his horse around" (nimmer wend' ich mein Rösslein um). He bids "Ade" to the setting sun and greets the "twinkling golden stars" (blinkenden Sterne Gold) that will serve as his guides. The stars are born wanderers, like the protagonist himself. The penultimate verse bids "Ade" to a mysterious "gleaming, bright window" (schimmerndes Fensterlein hell) that seems almost to invite him in. "Ah, I've ridden by so many times, and is today to be the last time? Good-bye!" (Vorüber, ach, ritt ich so manches Mal / Und wär' es denn heute zum letzten Mal? / Ade!). Again the music imposes a lockstep on the protagonist. He *must* cheerfully ride on, while the words hint at the mystery surrounding him. Is this the cottage of a lover or friend? Is it a symbol of lost love and opportunity, the "road not taken" in every life?

In the last verse the conflicting emotions the rider has worked so hard to suppress force themselves into the music, altering the tonality and dramatically softening the accompaniment. The listener is probably as astonished as the rider when he admits to himself how much he is leaving behind. He bids the stars "Ade" as they fade into gray, presumably as the new day nears. "You can't with all your numbers replace the little window's fading light, so what use are you if I must keep going? Good-bye stars, veil yourselves in gray! Good-bye!" No necessity in the world can silence "Sehnsucht." Nevertheless, the horse keeps galloping off into the distance of the postlude.

Marked "somewhat fast" (mässig geschwind), this song is often rushed, damaging its emotional and mimetic effects. The rider is trotting out of town and feeling very nostalgic about the place while he's doing it. He is not galloping energetically like the father in "Erlkönig."

The Heine Group

The German Jewish poet and essayist Heinrich Heine (1797–1856) may be best known to English-language readers for his chillingly prophetic statement "A country where books are burned, will burn people also." Aside from Goethe and Schiller, Heine is the greatest German poet set by Schubert. He felt profound ambivalence about his native land and even its language. Repelled by growing German nationalism and anti-

Semitism, Heine lived much of the later part of his life in France. His poetry expresses acute alienation and a bitter irony sharper even than that of Müller (whose work Heine admired). Heine's poetry, which Robert Schumann would later set extensively in many of his most important lieder, deals with disillusioned love with a cryptic concision new to romantic poetry. Heine is particularly famous for the "sting in the tail," the often surprising ironic twist that he frequently reserves for a poem's final line.

"Der Atlas" (Atlas)

> "Look at me, unhappy Atlas! I carry the world of sorrows. I wanted to be eternally happy or eternally wretched; so now, proud heart, you're wretched."

With "Der Atlas," a new expressive world seems to burst open from nowhere. The piano introduction is fast, flinty, jagged, expressionistic. This is an onslaught of emotion that seems to shake the boundaries of what can be expressed in coherent sound. The bass chords seem to sound from the bowels of the earth. "I am the unhappy Atlas! A world, the entire world of pain I must carry." This is not an epic hero of Beethovenian or Aeschylean mold, but an all too human man of the modern age, broken on a torturous wheel of his own making. The repetitions of "Ich unglücksel'ger Atlas!" hint at a pathologically exhibitionistic suffering. The enormity of the singer's burden is rendered memorably with the cutting E-flats on the repeated word "ganze" in the phrase "Die ganze Welt" (the whole world). " I bear the unbearable" (Ich trage Unerträgliches) is obsessively intoned, as if the weight of his anguish holds his voice in check until the next thought, "and my heart is going to break in my body" (und brechen / Will mir das Herz im Leibe), liberates the voice to surge to its highest point, the stinging F-sharp on "Leibe," the word stretched out over a truly crashing *fortissimo* that seems to threaten the continuation of the song. To be sure, hearts have been broken before in Western music, but it is arguable that never before has the metaphor been taken to such a realistic extreme.

The "break" is physically shattering to the music as the voice drops out for a few bars and a new, even more obsessive pattern emerges from the keyboard.

This awkward, violent syncopation given to the pianist marks the protagonist's tortured meditation in the central section of the song, his moment of tragic recognition. "You proud heart, you wanted it this way!" (Du stolzes Herz! du hast es ja gewollt!). The vocal line reflects his self-loathing with its jerky, militant rhythm: "You wanted to be happy, endlessly happy, or endlessly miserable" (Du wolltest glücklich sein, unendlich glücklich, / Oder unendlich elend). The word "end-lessly" (endlich) is drawn out by the singer with bitter irony on each repetition. "Proud heart, and now you're miserable" (stolzes Herz, / Und jetzo bist du elend). The recognition that he is indeed "miserable" (elend) is marked by a second shattering *fortissimo* and the piano transitions into the recapitulation of the song's opening lines, the words and their music intensified by all that has gone before. Even more than his identification with Atlas, the protagonist's realization of its implication, the "world of pain [he] must carry," drives the vocal line danger-ously over the stave for its highest notes on the final iteration of "Pain" (Schmerzen) to violent *fortissimo* chords in the piano. The volume is broken by a *piano* marking, suggesting that the turbulent keyboard figurations carry on *sotto voce* for four bars until a final *forte* chord ends the song. The beautifully molded dynamic shaping is respected by only a few recorded pianists, most of whom seem more interested is main-taining loudness than in Schubert's far subtler idea of dynamics whose rapid oscillations are unpredictable and rash, like the tortured mind to whom they give musical characterization.

"Ihr Bild" (Her Picture)

> *"I stand in dark dreams and stare at her picture. I can't believe I've lost you!"*

This is a song of more intimate confession than "Der Atlas," whose grinding *fortissimo* yields instantly at the start of "Ihr Bild" to a measure and a half of quiet bleakness; two notes resonate hollowly in *pianissimo* like two arresting, mysterious pulsations. This minimalism *avant la lettre*, the uncanny ability to summon a mood and scene before our imagination with the fewest preliminary notes is a Schubertian finger-print. For a second or two Schubert allows us the paradoxical experience of hearing silence. We are brought instantly to an interior setting of almost suffocating physical and psychological closeness.

"I stand in dark dreams and stare at her picture" (Ich stand in dunkeln Träumen, / Und starrt' ihr Bildnis an). The singer's line describes a droopy, sad melody that aspires upward only to sink into the depths. The effect mirrors the psychological experience of gazing at a lost loved one's picture; the grief often struggles with memories of former happiness. Heine's "stare" (starrt'), however, hints at a mental state more troubling than mere nostalgia, and Schubert's briefly dragging, dissonant setting of the word ensures we register the moment of dumbstruck stasis. The same note colors the first syllable of the object of the "stare," her "picture" (Bildnis). The piano alone now echoes the voice in its more sepulchral depths. "And the beloved face mysteriously started to come to life." The singer's line now strives upward, the precarious illusion creating a crescendo and keeping the voice from sagging as before. The beloved's "face" (Antlitz) is brightly set while the singer's reference to the "mysterious" (heimlich) way the face comes to life lifts the voice to his highest note in the song, a precarious joy only attainable for the singer in lonely fantasy. The keyboard again echoes the singer, closing the song's first section with a similarly brightened response.

The *pianissimo* marking returns, as the singer describes, to new music, the beloved's lips appearing "to smile wonderfully" while "it seems her eyes sparkle with sad tears" (Und wie von Wehmutstränen / Erglänzte ihr Augenpaar). In this poem, Heine delivers his famous "stings" in abundance, not even waiting for the final tag, and Schubert makes them musically visceral. The woman's face and its "wonderful smile" (Lächeln wunderbar) is set sweetly, an almost cloying effect if it weren't for the hollow, sepulchral harmonies in both the vocal and keyboard writing. The rather incongruous "sad tears" (Wehmutstränen) hints at the lost woman's own potential anguish, despite the smiling mouth and sparkling eyes. "Wehmutstränen" is set to funereal descending notes, suggesting her smiling sadness is something more than the conventional sentimental melancholy implied by many translations. The singer's exquisite trill on "eyes" (Augen) is filled with tenderness.

Now follows nearly three measures of solo piano; the mysterious, hollow pulsation returns, while the harmony gropes torturously back toward the song's initial key, marking the recapitulation and the singer's tragic reversal and recognition. "My tears are flowing down my cheeks as well" (Auch meine Tränen flossen / Mir von den Wangen herab). The ambiguous tears of the portrait are now the singer's tears, as the opening *pianissimo* melody and accompaniment return. Again the piano echoes the voice in a brief solo response from its hollow depths. "And ah! I cannot believe that I have lost you!" (Und ach, ich kann es nicht glauben, / Dass ich dich verloren hab'!). Both "believe" (glauben) and "you" (dich) are musically heightened with the same piercing notes that accented "face" and "mysterious," only now the mood, affected by all that has gone before, is one of crushing loss. The crescendo during "I can't believe I've lost you!" and the following bars of keyboard writing give the song a bitter finality.

"Das Fischermädchen" (The Fisher Girl)

"You lovely fisher girl, row your boat to shore and we'll cuddle hand in hand. Every day you trust yourself to the raging sea. My heart is just like it."

The standard opinion on "Das Fischermädchen" is that the same Schubert who wrote the other Heine settings momentarily lost his ability to appreciate the poet's insinuating irony and created instead a sunny, wistful song that does little justice to the poem. The standard reactions of *audiences* to a good performance of "Das Fischermädchen" is that it is one of the loveliest of all German songs, contrasting ingeniously with its fellows in the Heine set. The innocence of tone and purity of execution can move the listener to tears, in no small measure because of the song's placement amid such dark works of disillusion and despair.

Heine seems to be offering an ironic image of a jaded sophisticate seeking love in all the wrong places—in this case an illiterate peasant girl, a sort of Don Giovanni/Zerlina scenario. Schubert offers steadily pulsing, serene water music in the keyboard writing, hinting at a natural order at peace with itself and an ingratiating vocal melody that seems to come directly from folk song. Schubert affords us a prelapsarian paradise of desire and invitation. This innocence too is part of love and desire, the themes that link all of *Schwanengesang*. This innocence is all the more beautiful for its very fragility. The singer's opening phrase,"You lovely fisher girl, row your boat to shore" (Du schönes Fischermädchen, / Treibe den Kahn ans Land) comprises a rising arc of notes, making audible his gesture to the girl and the aspiration of his longing. The keyboard pleads along with the singer in a phrase of ringing, ascending chords that punctuate the song. The next phrase, "come and sit by me and we'll cuddle hand in hand" (Komm zu mir und setze dich nieder, / Wir kosen Hand in Hand), one of the most endearing lines of German poetry imaginable, is set to music of incomparable sweetness. Particularly memorable is the lovely trill on the last repetition of "Hand," expressing the thrill of their anticipated physical contact.

Now the keyboard writing becomes softer as the singer's words grow even more intimate and seductive. "Lay your little head on my heart and don't be too afraid; every day you trust yourself fearlessly to the wild sea." The vocal melody is a close variant of the main tune. Its most prominent device is an adorable rising of pitch on the phrase "don't be too afraid" (fürchte dich nicht zu sehr), which is immediately echoed by the piano's earlier phrase of rising, ringing chords seeming to sweep away all apprehension. "Fearlessly" (sorglos) is treated to a confident upward-moving decoration and the "wild sea" (wilden Meer) receives a ringing delivery reaching above the stave. Surely the singer can't be more dangerous than the sea itself! The accompaniment swells again with its steady barcarolle tune, softening for the singer's final blandishment, sung to the opening vocal melody, bringing this jewel of a song to its conclusion. "My heart is like the sea, it's got its storms and ebbs and flows, and many beautiful pearls lie in its depths." The "storms and ebbs and flows" are followed by those ingratiating rising chords from the pianist. Again they serve to drive away apprehension, and perhaps also drive the girl closer, into the singer's arms. The "depths" (Tiefe) of the singer's heart receive the same notes and trill as graced "Hand," and the song trails away with the piano's quieting pulsation.

Schubert's often tragic perspective is only one aspect of his staggeringly comprehensive view of life. So much of his vision revolves around the quest for love, however impossible that may have seemed as his brief life progressed. Ironically, he might have found life easier to endure if he had permanently adopted the hardened ironic shell of a Heine or a later romantic composer such as Hugo Wolf. It is to our benefit that he retained his capacity for emotional openness even to the end.

"Die Stadt" (The City)

> *"On the far horizon it appears, like a cloud picture, the city with its towers, in the evening twilight. With a mournful rhythm the boatman rows my boat. The sun rises again and shows me that place, where I lost my love!"*

This song creates another shock of contrast. The piece opens with five and a half bars of solo keyboard that couples a muffled *pianissimo* drumbeat with a rapid up-and-down swirling pattern—the sonic embodiment of the boat's ominous gliding and the water rippling along its sides in response to the boatman's oars. Schubert's songs are filled with images of water and boats. But here the C minor tonality (the same as the contemporary, death-obsessed sonata, D. 958), the fatalism of the steady notes heard through their haze of pedal, create not so much a proto-impressionistic image of the natural world, which Schubert had achieved before, but a full-fledged expressionistic vision. If there are other passengers on Heine's boat, they are experiencing a routine commuter trip. Schubert's protagonist, however, stands like Orpheus or Dante on the boat to the underworld.

The natural flow of the piano's ghostly water music comes almost to a full stop save for a single note in the bass before the voice enters. This unnatural halt of the music's flow suggests that the singer has just seen the "cloud picture" (Nebelbild). The momentary silence implies that his consciousness is the true focal point of all that surrounds him.

As in a painting by Van Gogh or Egon Schiele, everything emanates from that tortured consciousness. Not even *Winterreise* attained this level of subjectivity. The voice is directed to sing "softly" as the first, eerily static theme commences, the piano accompanying with emphatic chords. "On the distant horizon it appears, like a cloud image" (Am fernen Horizonte / Erscheint, wie ein Nebelbild). The vocal melody clings to G and then A-flat, suggesting the singer's fixed stare. The vocal line climbs to E-flat for another succession of static notes as the singer's gaze travels up to the emerging towers catching "the light of the setting sun" (In Abenddämmrung gehüllt). The keyboard introduction is reiterated, with its muffled pulsation resolving into the arabesques of rhythmically churning gray water. This time the voice is allowed to float above these strangely menacing swirls as the singer's second melody, a listlessly drooping theme, serves to describe the cold wind, the rippling water, and the boatman's "mournful rhythm" (traurigem Takte). The keyboard swirling suggests that the boatman is picking up his rowing pace now that the city is in view. The swirls continue without the singer for nearly two measures before the rowing evidently stops and the muffled pulsation returns. Is the boat gliding in to dock?

Another disconcertingly unnatural pause all but silences the water music save for that single note in the bass. The singer's original vocal theme returns nearly unchanged to clinch the drama: "The sun rises once more shining from the earth, and shows me that place where I lost my love" (Die Sonne hebt sich noch einmal / Leuchtend von Boden empor, / Und zeigt mir jene Stelle, / Wo ich das Liebste verlor). Now the vocal line is declaimed "strongly" as the singer masochistically confronts the briefly radiant scene of his undoing before the dying sputter of sunlight leaves the "twilight-shaded city." The accompaniment returns to supportive chords played with greater vehemence than before. The vocal line rises to a shattering G, the highest in the song, on the all-important word, "Liebste" (beloved). With the confrontation of the protagonist, the place, and his past, the singing stops and the ghostly water music resumes, as much an expression of the singer's mind as a phenomenon of his outer world. Again the mysterious muffled pulsation. The sound of the gliding boat? Or some symbol of fate, like the

drumbeats in a Mahler symphony? Again the swirls of grayish water, a
rest, a single low note in the bass, and then silence.

"Am Meer" (By the Sea)

> *"The sea sparkled in the last glow of evening. We sat by a fisher-*
> *man's house, silent and alone. The fog rose up, the water swelled;*
> *tears flowed from your loving eyes. I saw them falling, and I sank*
> *on my knee, drinking the tears from your white hand. Since that*
> *hour my body wastes away from desire; you wretched woman, you've*
> *poisoned me with your tears."*

This is perhaps Schubert's most personal song. The poem alone is a
work of profound ambivalence. Who is this couple? Why are they here?
What has just transpired? Why is the woman crying? Conventional love
poetry often speaks of a lover wasting away from desire, but here the
tears the man has "drunk" are a "poison" that attacks the soul as well.
Whatever Heine is getting at with his stinging irony, there should be
no avoiding what Schubert saw in this poem. It embodies a moment of a
deeply ambivalent transaction between a man and a "wretched woman,"
resulting in the mortal infection of the dying protagonist. This is the
enacting and recognition scene of Schubert's own most intimate tragedy, where eros and thanatos conjoined. One recalls the composer's
postinfection aversion to any talk of marriage and his supposed disdain
for women in later life. The words and their setting are filled with
horror and justifiable self-pity, but there is no hatred expressed for the
"miserable" or "hapless woman" (unglücksel'ge Weib). Only weeks after
composing this song, when his final illness struck him, Schubert was
convinced that he had been "poisoned" by some fish he had ordered at
an inn with his friends. Baron Schönstein, an amateur singer and one
of his best interpreters during his lifetime, recalled that the composer
"was frequently seized with the idea that he had taken poison," vividly
recalling Schubert during one of his stays at Zselíz. "He no longer had
a moment's peace and on the evening before my return to Vienna—I
was also visiting Zselíz, on leave—he besought me to take him with
me. So we traveled together and arrived safe and sound in Vienna

and perfectly well. That was at the beginning of September; Schubert ought not to have left Zselíz until November, *with* the Esterházy family" (Deutsch 1958, 101–102). Schönstein could not remember the year of this incident. Whenever it happened, the singer's recollections suggest that "poison" was a debilitating phobia for the composer. If, as seems likely, it was during Schubert's 1824 stay at Zselíz, the phobia seems linked to his syphilitic infection and perhaps the mercury treatments to which he was subjected.

Marked "very slow," "Am Meer" begins with four chords setting the scene, a vision of stasis where contentment is initially hard to differentiate from sadness. The main vocal theme and its chordal accompaniment are richly hymnal, suggesting the "last glow of evening" (letzten Abendscheine) and the couple's rapt, mysterious stillness. It is "glowing" music, yet tinged with an indescribable sadness. Is this a hymn to the singer's last moment of intimacy with another human being? The solemn stillness proves illusory as the keyboard almost imperceptibly segues into a passage of muted, threatening tremolo. The fog has risen, the sea is swelling, and the gulls are moving restlessly, as against some storm. The unease in nature is only mirroring a far more ambiguous emotional transaction between the couple. As the tremolo and crescendo subside, the woman's "eyes full of love" (Augen liebevoll) begin to overflow. Tears of grief? Of pity? Happiness? This unspeaking woman is the most mysterious "other" in all of Schubert's songs. To the strains of the opening melody, the singer describes watching the tears fall and his impulsive "drinking" (fortgetrunken) of the "tears" (Tränen) from her "white hand" (weissen Hand). The "tears" rest on two high Fs at the top of the stave. Now the tremolo sounds of threatening nature return, but the storm has decidedly shifted to the interior life of the protagonist. The singer and his accompaniment again rise in agitation as he describes his physical and spiritual destruction. The song ends with a brief reprise of the hymn as the protagonist makes his fateful discovery, that the miserable woman has poisoned him with her tears. The final word, "Tränen," is subjected to a measure-long oscillating decoration, surely the most heartbreaking ornamentation in Schubert's vocal music. It is mournful, yet drawn out with a sensuous longing. The four opening chords return, only to fade into nothingness.

"Der Doppelgänger" (Deathly Double) (CD Track 20)

> *"The night is still, the streets are quiet, in this house dwelt my love;*
> *it's a long time since she left the city, but the house still stands in*
> *the same square. Another man is standing there also, and wrings*
> *his hands, overwhelmed with suffering; I shudder when I see his*
> *face; the moon shows me my own image. You ghostly double! Why*
> *do you ape my love sufferings that troubled me here so many nights*
> *in times gone by?"*

In "Der Doppelgänger," the denouement of "Am Meer" is played out. All
the tragic power of *King Lear* or *Woyzeck* is miraculously compressed
into two pages of score. The poem, like all the Heine works, is powerfully effective as text alone. What Schubert does with these words is no
less miraculous than Berg's musical elaboration of Büchner's *Woyzeck*
into *Wozzeck* or Verdi's translation of Shakespeare's Falstaff plays and
Othello into his own late idiom. The song's key of B minor links it with
the "Unfinished" Symphony of 1822, conceived during the fateful period
of Schubert's infection. "Doppelgänger" opens new expressive possibilities in the portrayal of a tortured subjectivity. Whether consciously or
not, Schubert's return to B minor here "closes the book" on his illness
and his life.

Marked "very slow," the song opens with four stark bars of keyboard
writing (0:00–0:16). The soft chords are hollow, unearthly, creating a
sense of the uncanny in a matter of seconds. It is no accident that they
also present a variant of the Gregorian chant *Dies irae*, describing the
day of judgment for the faithful Catholic. What is to come is surely a
final reckoning. "The night is still" (Still ist die Nacht), intones the voice
in four static, droning F-sharps (0:17–0:24). The rest of the opening
sentence, "the streets are quiet; in this house dwelt my love," hovers on
that F-sharp but dips repeatedly into the voice's lower regions, indulg-
ing in mournful decorations reminiscent of the arabesques that make
Jewish cantorial singing so moving (0:25–0:51). The keyboard solo
response to the phrase (0:52–0:59) makes the most ghostly of echoes.
The next line (1:01), "It's a long time since she left the city, but the
house still stands in the same square," is set to a melodic variant on the
first, deepening the gloom. The ornamentation on "the same [square]"

(demselben; 1:26–1:30) highlights the sense of uncanny stasis. Again we hear the piano's ghostly, if incomplete echo (1:36–1:42).

Now, in the middle section of the song (1:50), the music begins a crescendo, "bit by bit" (*poco a poco*). The vocal line begins a slow but unnerving climb up the stave. "Another man is standing there also, staring upward and wringing his hands, overwhelmed with suffering." "Overwhelmed with suffering" (vor Schmerzensgewalt) is sung and played to a shuddering *fortissimo* (2:07) made all the more unnerving by the sudden decrescendo demanded for the singer and the pianist. In two quiet, reflective bars (2:20) the singer recoils in recognition, "I shudder" (Mir graust es), as he and the piano begin the ascent toward the most terrifying crescendo in all of Schubert's songs: "when I see his face; the moon shows me my own image." "My own image" (meine eigne Gestalt; 2:41–2:49) lifts the voice in triple *forte* to its highest note in the song, the climactic moment in this particular song drama and of Schubert's entire song literature. Unlike the miller boy or the winter wanderer, this doppelgänger will not die or suffer madness in its creator's stead. It is a moment of self-recognition as terrifying as that found in Sophocles's *Oedipus the King*, but Schubert has managed it all within the span not of thousands of lines and two hours of stage time but of a mere forty bars of music.

A brief moment of decrescendo in the piano part (2:50) serves to preface the final quickening of musical pulse: the final crescendo, the final reckoning between the protagonist and his ghostly image, a premonition of death with roots deep in Germanic folklore. "You ghostly double, you pale fellow!" (Du Doppelgänger! du bleicher Geselle!; 2:52). Structurally we are at a recapitulation of the song's opening words, the voice cleaving to F-sharp for all but one syllable. That single lift to A on "fellow" (Geselle) suggests the singer's futile mockery, a whistling past the graveyard. As tempo and volume inexorably build (3:02), the singer desperately asks, "Why do you ape my love sufferings that troubled me at this very place?" A rest is followed by a powerful chord, another rest, then the entire agony of the protagonist's life (and the composer's as well) finds expression (3:15–3:36) in the setting for "so many nights in times gone by" (So manche Nacht, in alter Zeit?). "So many nights" is set to wrenching *fortissimos*, as if both the voice and the comparatively fragile keyboard of the early nineteenth century have been brought to their breaking point under the burden of this sorrow. But the rage against the loss of love and the dying of the light is short-lived. Again the demand for a sudden decrescendo begins as the voice makes the saddest of its cantorial-like arabesques over "alter" in the phrase "times gone by." The voice is silenced while the keyboard plays on for seven bars of increasingly gentle, desolate chords (3:36–3:59) until the work comes to silence.

For all its strangeness, "Der Doppelgänger," like several of the other Heine settings, is in fundamentally an ABA pattern. The nightmarish proto-expressionism of the song can easily put listeners off their bearings. To paraphrase Liszt, Schubert's emotional power is so great as to blind us to his extraordinary craft and sense of form.

The Final Seidl Song

"Die Taubenpost" (The Pigeon Post)

> *"I have a carrier pigeon who conveys love notes to my beloved. The name of the bird? It's Longing. Do you know it?"*

Schubert could not have written a more perfect farewell to song than "Die Taubenpost," nor could there be a more satisfying resolution for the cycle's audience after the shattering power of "Der Doppelgänger." At first glance, this song sits comfortably within the "gemütlich" milieu of the Biedermeier drawing room. But the music's ingratiating beauty lifts Seidl's comfortable, time-tested sentiments to a level of sublimity. The song celebrates the most ephemeral of lyrics and stock poetical conceits while at the same time breaching the boundaries of the art song, allowing the composer, in the last verse, to address his audience directly at what would prove to be the end of his career, offering an apologia for his life and art. For Schubert and his audiences, the faithful bird is Schubert's creative inspiration, made up of love and longing. Its ultimate reward is not, nor could be materially recompensed. It is enough that we preserve it "truly in [our] breast." The name of the "Taubenpost," and of Schubert's central inspiration, is "Sehnsucht," Longing, a name known to all people, and especially all lovers of Schubert's music.

The song follows an ABAC structure. It is marked "somewhat slow." Surely the delightfully syncopated music should dance off the page in performance, but it is a graceful and sweet kind of dancing, the tempo indication allowing the performers the breathing space to tug at the listener's heart. It is music of longing but also full of optimism. The love expressed *will* be returned, if only in the exchange among composer, performers, and audience in an eternal act of communion. The many details in "Die Taubenpost" grow on the listener's affections as in virtually no other song. The way the keyboard doubles the vocal line on "many beloved places" (manchem lieben Ort) is almost as breathtaking as the little keyboard figure that manages to both glow and flutter like the eager "Taubenpost" on mention of the bird's arrival "at the beloved's house" (Bis zu der Liebsten Haus), the declaration, "The bird is so true to me!" (Die Taub' ist so mir treu!), and "the messenger of faithful minds" (Die Botin treuen Sinns). As in "Liebesbotschaft," there are magical passages of transition for the keyboard between verses, especially when the opening music is recapitulated before "By day, by night, in waking, in dream" (Bei Tag, bei Nacht, in Wachen, in Traum).

The song's coda makes up one of the most remarkable pages in song literature. It is built out of the answer and musical elaboration of the poem's riddle. The urgent repetitions and the use of rests are highly suggestive for the singer. "Her name—[rest] is Longing! [rest—rest] Do you know her?—[rest—rest] Do you know her? The messenger of faithful minds. [rest] The messenger of faithful minds" (Sie heisst—die Sehnsucht! Kennt ihr sie?—Die Botin treuen Sinns). Graham Johnson observes, "The music seems to scan the face of the person to whom the question is addressed ('Do you know it . . . *do you?* . . . please tell me!'). 'Die Botin treuen Sinns' is full of the greatest tenderness, as well as pride. These birds are the narrator's life and love" (1989–97, 37: 108). A fine singing actor such as Hans Hotter can realize the effect Johnson is describing, suggesting to listeners even through the medium of audio recording that the song's protagonist, and through him the composer, is directly speaking to us. In concert, the impression is even more direct. The effect is similar to the feeling audiences have long had that Shakespeare is speaking directly to them through the figure of Prospero in the epilogue of his last play, *The Tempest*, pleading to be "set free" and that his "project" was simply "to please."

Just a few years before Schubert wrote this song, Beethoven had similarly "spoken" to his audience when the chorus in his Ninth Symphony addressed contemporary and all future audiences with the cry of "Brüder!" (Brothers!). Schubert's love of the older composer's work was profound, and he paid Beethoven's music the compliment of virtually never attempting to imitate it. From his earliest works, Schubert sought his own way as a composer, and it is one of the greatest triumphs of art that without the benefit of Beethoven's fame, international acceptance, and much longer life span, he achieved a comparable musical legacy. Something of this miracle can be glimpsed in this last song, written sometime in October 1828, a matter of days before the onset of the composer's last illness. Schubert's music, like the carrier pigeon, lives always in "faithful hearts"; he speaks to all our deepest longings, fears, and nostalgia and hopes to be enveloped somehow in a love that has no end. Like Bach's "Jesu Joy of Man's Desiring," "Die Taubenpost" gives the feeling that it has never ended and can never end. It continues just out of our hearing, resonating long after the performance is over.

*   *   *   *

Schubert is the most personal of the great masters, and this may allow me the freedom for a personal confession. If I had only one hour of life left to give to music, I can think of no other work to better spend it with than with this "accidental" cycle, which, like Schubert's work as a whole, embodies the entirety of human experience and all the mysterious forces that he perceived as animating the world around humankind. Where else can we go from the horrific to the homely, the godlike to the pathetic, to experience the fullest range of spring colors and the bleakest vistas of winter, the babbling brook, and the very sound of silence itself?

Selected Discography
and Videography

Collections

The *Hyperion Schubert Song Edition* is the first complete recording of all of Schubert's songs including the surviving fragments. Available in thirty-seven individual volumes or as a boxed set, its standards of performance are very high. The annotations by the series director and accompanist, Graham Johnson, are excellent and detailed. Particularly fine contributions are made by Brigitte Fassbaender, Lucia Popp, Peter Schreier, and Ian Bostridge, whose version of *Die Schöne Müllerin* established his career as a lieder singer. One recurrent criticism is that the majority of the singers are British and that the German diction is not always as authentic as possible. The budget label Naxos is assembling its own complete edition. The artists used are all native German speakers, hence its title, the *Deutsche Schubert-Lied-Edition*. Directed by the pianists Stefan Laux and Ulrich Eisenlohr, the Naxos series makes this huge legacy available in good versions to an even larger audience. The documentation is good.

Dietrich Fischer-Dieskau's recording from the late 1960s and early 1970s of some four hundred songs, roughly all the male-voice lieder, accompanied by Gerald Moore on twenty-one Deutsche Grammophon CDs, is another recording milestone and an excellent way to acquire a large selection of songs with full translations. This is a prodigious feat of interpretation by a great singer and accompanist who sustain a high level of excellence. Their art is perhaps best represented, however, by their earlier recordings, which have been reissued on EMI. These earlier interpretations are fresher and less studied than the DG versions. Hermann Prey's recordings of some fifty lieder plus the three cycles have been available sporadically from Philips and represent a monument of great Schubert interpretation. Siegfried Lorenz is a fine baritone who has a representative collection of the songs and cycles accompanied by Norman Shetler on Berlin Classics.

Elly Ameling on Philips recorded some four CDs' worth of Schubert that represents the strongest large collection of female songs. Often characterized as a light, "delectable" soprano, she plumbs the depths of "Gretchen am Spinnrade" as well as anyone. Gundula Janowitz's four discs on DG are also good, if less dramatically involving. (This was going to be a "women's songs" collection to balance Fischer-Dieskau's, but the company abandoned the project halfway through.) The part songs like "Nachthelle" can be found in the Warner Classics complete set of Secular Choral Works by the Arnold Schoenberg Choir or a more selective compilation of these works led by Wolfgang Sawallisch on EMI.

The Cycles

Die Schöne Müllerin. Probably most effective when sung by a tenor voice: Aksel Schiøtz (Danacord), Julius Patzak (Preiser), Fritz Wunderlich (DG), Peter Schreier (Decca or Berlin Classics), Ian Bostridge (Hyperion). My favorite version is hard to find at the moment: Ernst Haefliger with Jacqueline Bonneau on DG in 1960, only available in a large collection of that singer's work issued in Japan. The best baritone version is Hermann Prey's on Philips. Mezzo Brigitte Fassbaender offers an insightful version on DG. The best current DVD offers Fischer-Dieskau near the end of his career with the fine accompaniment of Christoph Eschenbach on EMI, filmed by Bruno Monsaingeon.

Winterreise. Among tenors: Peter Anders (DG), Peter Schreier (with Sviatoslav Richter on Philips), Peter Pears and Benjamin Britten (Decca). A very beautiful live version by an elderly Ernst Haefliger is available from Japan on the Camerata label. Baritones: Hermann Prey (EMI), Fischer-Dieskau (with Moore on EMI mono, and with Alfred Brendel on Philips), Roman Trekel (Naxos). Bass-baritones: Hans Hotter with Moore (on EMI) and Werba (DG). Bass: Kurt Moll (Orfeo). There are good DVD versions of Fischer-Dieskau with Brendel and Thomas Quasthoff with Barenboim. Mezzo Brigitte Fassbaender's audio recording on EMI is perhaps the most intense version of all, but her DVD version regrettably shows little of her and focuses on the imaginative exploits of the director. The fine singer Ian Bostridge's DVD is unfortunately undermined by the director's mawkish concept. Peter Pears and Benjamin Britten's DVD also offers an unsatisfying "staging" but includes a brief, fascinating "bonus" feature of the two artists discussing the work, shot in 1968.

Schwanengesang. Brigitte Fassbaender (DG), Peter Schreier (Decca), Hans Hotter (EMI), Fischer-Dieskau and Brendel (Philips). Hopefully, Hermann Prey's excellent filmed performance with Leonard Hokanson will appear on DVD. Prey filmed all three cycles with Hokanson for Unitel as well as a large amount of Schubert for Japanese television during the Indian summer of his career; all have yet to appear.

Schubert Recitals

Ian Bostridge with Julius Drake: *Schubert Lieder* Volumes I and II on EMI.

Brigitte Fassbaender and Erik Werba: *Lieder Vol. 2* (with lieder by Wolf) on German EMI.

Brigitte Fassbaender and Cord Garben: *Goethe Songs* on Sony.

Dietrich Fischer-Dieskau and Jörg Demus: *Goethe Lieder* on DG.

An excellent late recital of selected lieder with Fischer-Dieskau is appended to Bruno Monsaingeon's documentary on the singer, *Autumn Journey*, on DVD.

Ernst Haefliger: *21 Lieder* on Claves.

Marjana Lipovšek: *Schubert Lieder* on Orfeo.

Kurt Moll: *Schubert Lieder for Bass* on Orfeo.

Jessye Norman and Philip Moll: *Schubert Lieder* on Philips.

Lucia Popp with Irwin Gage: *Schubert Lieder* on EMI.

Hermann Prey: Goethe and Schiller songs with Moore in *Hermann Prey: Lieder Vol. 1* on EMI.

Christine Schäfer: *Schubert Lieder* on Orfeo.

Peter Schreier: recitals with Walter Olbertz will hopefully emerge from Berlin Classics.

Elisabeth Schumann: *Schubert Lieder* on Naxos.

Elisabeth Schwarzkopf with Edwin Fischer: *Schubert 24 Lieder* on EMI.

Irmgard Seefried: lieder recordings on DG, Testament, and other labels.

Mitsuko Shirai: *Schubert Lieder* on Capriccio.

Elisabeth Söderström and Paul Badura-Skoda (playing an instrument of Schubert's time): *Goethe Lieder* on Astrée.

Cheryl Studer: *Schubert Lieder* on DG.

Historic recordings with Gerhard Hüsch, Karl Erb, Heinrich Rehkemper, Heinrich Schlussnuss, Ria Ginster, and Elena Gerhardt. Most of these great artists are included in EMI's two-volume *Schubert Lieder on Record* collection.

Bibliography

Badura-Skoda, Paul. 2007. *Être musicien*. Paris: Hermann.

Baumann, Cecilia C. 1981. *Wilhelm Müller: The Poet of the Schubert Song Cycles: His Life and Works*. University Park: Pennsylvania State University Press.

Bie, Oscar. 1971. *Schubert the Man*. Westport, Connecticut: Greenwood Press.

Black, Leo. 2003. *Franz Schubert: Music and Belief*. Rochester, New York: Boydell Press

————. 1997. *Wort oder Ton?* Can a native English speaker ever hope to appreciate the *Lied*? *The Musical Times* (March): 21–27.

Botstein, Leon. 1977. Realism transformed: Franz Schubert and Vienna. In *The Cambridge Companion to Schubert*. Ed. Christopher Gibbs. Cambridge: Cambridge University Press, 1997. 15–35.

Brendel, Alfred. *Schubert's Late Piano Works*. 5 DVDs. European Union: Euroarts, 2007.

Brown, Jane K. 2004. In the beginning was poetry. In *The Cambridge Companion to the Lied*. Ed. James Parsons. Cambridge: Cambridge University Press. 12–34.

————. 1997. The poetry of Schubert's songs. In *Schubert's Vienna*. Ed. Raymond Erickson. New Haven: Yale University Press. 183–213.

Brown, Maurice J. 1966. *Essays on Schubert*. London: St. Martin's Press.

————. 1958. *Schubert: A Critical Biography*. London: Macmillan.

————. 1967. *Schubert Songs*. London: A British Broadcasting Corporation publication.

Capell, Richard. 1957. *Schubert's Songs*. London: Pan Books.

Chusud, Martin, ed. 2000. *A Companion to Schubert's* Schwanengesang: *History, Poets, Analysis, Performance*. New Haven: Yale University Press.

Clive, Peter. 1997. *Schubert and His World: A Biographical Dictionary*. Oxford: Clarendon Press.

Deutsch, Otto Erich. 1977. *Schubert: A Documentary Biography.* Trans.
Eric Blom. New York: Da Capo Press.

———. 1958. *Schubert: Memoirs by His Friends.* London: Adam and
Charles Black.

Dittrich, Marie-Agnes. 2004. The lieder of Schubert. In *The Cambridge
Companion to the Lied.* Ed. James Parsons. Cambridge: Cambridge
University Press. 85–100.

Erickson, Raymond. 1997. Vienna in its European context. In *Schubert's
Vienna.* Ed. Raymond Erickson. New Haven: Yale University Press.

Fassbaender, Brigitte. 1995. A personal note on *Die Schöne Müllerin.*
Booklet for her CD recording. Deutsche Grammophon. 2–4.

———. 1997. A statement on Franz Schubert's 200th birthday. *Österreichische Musikzeitschrift,* Schubert Special. English-language version. Vienna. 12.

Fischer-Dieskau, Dietrich. 1978. *Schubert's Songs: A Biographical Study.*
Trans. Kenneth S. Whitton. New York: Knopf.

Gilroy Bevan, Peter. 1998. Adversity: Schubert's illnesses and their
background. In *Schubert Studies.* Ed. Brian Newbould. Brookfield,
Vermont: Ashgate. 244–66.

Giarusso, Richard. 2008. Beyond the Leiermann: Disorder, reality, and
the power of imagination in the final songs of Schubert's *Winterreise.*
In *The Unknown Schubert.* Ed. Barbara M. Reul and Lorraine Byrne
Bodley. Burlington, Vermont: Ashgate.

Goethe, Johann Wolfgang von. 1966. *Goethe: Conversations and Encoun-
ters.* Ed. and trans. David Luke and Robert Pick. Chicago: Henry
Regnery Company.

Gramit, David. 1997. "The passion for friendship": music, cultivation,
and identity in Schubert's circle. In *The Cambridge Companion to
Schubert.* Ed. Christopher Gibbs. Cambridge: Cambridge University
Pres. 56–71.

Hilmar, Ernst. 1988. Franz Schubert in His Time. Portland, Oregon:
Amadeus Press.

———. 1996. *Schubert.* Graz: Akademische Druck und Verlagsanstalt.

Hirsch, Marjorie Wing. 1993. *Schubert's Dramatic Lieder.* Cambridge:
Cambridge University Press.

Johnson, Graham. 1989–97. Program notes to the *Hyperion Schubert
Edition,* Vols. 1–34. London: Hyperion Records.

Johnson, Paul. 1991. *The Birth of the Modern: World Society 1815–1830*. New York: HarperCollins.

Klein, Rudolf. 1972. *Schubert Stätten*. Vienna: Verlag Elisabeth Lafite.

Kramer, Lawrence. 1998. *Franz Schubert: Sexuality, Subjectivity, Song*. Cambridge: Cambridge University Press.

Kramer, Richard. 1994. *Distant Cycles: Schubert and the Conceiving of Song*. Chicago: University of Chicago Press.

Lehmann, Lotte. 1972. *Eighteen Song Cycles: Studies in Their Interpretation*. New York: Praeger.

———. 1985. *More Than Singing: The Interpretation of Songs*. New York: Dover.

McCay, Elizabeth Norman. 1996. *Schubert: A Biography*. Oxford: Oxford University Press.

Messing, Scott. 2006. *Schubert in the European Imagination. Volume I: The Romantic and Victorian Eras*. Eastman Studies in Music. Rochester, New York: University of Rochester Press.

———. 2007. *Schubert in the European Imagination. Volume 2: Fin-de-Siècle Vienna*. Eastman Studies in Music. Rochester, New York: University of Rochester Press.

Moore, Gerald. 1962. *Am I Too Loud?* New York: Macmillan.

———. 1978. *Farewell Recital: Further Memoirs*. New York: Taplinger.

———. 1975. *The Schubert Song Cycles: With Thoughts on Performance*. London: Hamish.

———. *The Unashamed Accompanist*. 1999. Testament CD SBT 1176.

Muxfeldt, Kristina. 1997. Schubert's songs: the transformation of a genre. In *The Cambridge Companion to Schubert*. Ed. Christopher H. Gibbs. Cambridge: Cambridge University Press. 121–37.

Newbould, Brian. 1997. *Schubert: The Music and the Man*. Berkeley: University of California Press.

———, ed. 2003. *Schubert the Progressive: History, Performance Practice, Analysis*. Burlington, Vermont: Ashgate.

Osborne, Charles. 1985. *Schubert and His Vienna*. New York: Knopf.

Parsons, James. 2004. Introduction: why the lied? In *The Cambridge Companion to the Lied*. Ed. James Parsons. Cambridge: Cambridge University Press. 3–11.

Prey, Hermann. 1986. *First Night Fever: The Memoirs of Hermann Prey.* Trans. Andrew Shackelton. New York: Riverrun Press.

Reed, John. 1987. *Schubert.* London: J. M. Dent and Sons.

————. 1972. *Schubert: The Final Years.* London: Faber and Faber.

————. 1985. *The Schubert Song Companion.* New York: Universe Books.

Reverter, Arturo. 1999. *Schubert: Lieder Completos.* Barcelona: Ediciones Península.

Ruppert, Frank. 2007. *Franz Schubert and the Rose Cross Mystery.* Pittsburgh, Pennsylvania: Rose Dog Books.

Sadie, Julie Anne, and Stanley Sadie. 2005. *Calling on the Composer: A Guide to European Composer Houses and Museums.* New Haven: Yale University Press.

Schiller, Friedrich. 1965. *On the Aesthetic Education of Man.* Trans. with an introduction by Reginald Snell. New York: Frederick Unger.

Schubert, Franz. 1970. *Franz Schubert's Letters and Other Writings.* Ed. Otto Erich Deutsch. Trans. Venetia Savile. Freeport, New York: Books for Libraries Press.

————. 1992. *Schubert: The Complete Song Texts.* Trans. Richard Wigmore. London: Victor Gollancz.

Schumann, Elisabeth. 1948. *German Song.* New York: Chanticleer Press.

Solomon, Maynard. 1989. Franz Schubert and the peacocks of Benvenuto Cellini. *19th Century Music* 12: 193–206.

————. 1981. Franz Schubert's *"Mein Traum." American Imago* 38: 137–54.

Steblin, Rita. 1993. The peacock's tale: Schubert's sexuality reconsidered. *19th Century Music* 17: 5–33.

————. 1997. Schubert through the kaleidoscope: The "Unsinnsgesellshaft" and its illustrious members. In *Österreichische Musikzeitschrift,* Schubert Special. English-language version. Vienna. 52–61.

————. 2008. Schubert's Pepi: his love affair with the chambermaid Josepha Pöcklhofer and her surprising fate. *The Musical Times* 149: 47–69.

————. 2001. Schubert's problematic relationship with Johann Mayrhofer: new documentary evidence. In *Essays on Music and Culture in Honor of Herbert Kellman.* Ed. Barbara Haggh. Paris: Minerva. 465–95.

————. 1998. Schubert's relationship with women: an historical account. In *Schubert Studies*. Ed. Brian Newbould. Brookfield, Vermont: Ashgate. 220–43.

———— with Friederick Stocken. 2007. Studying with Sechter: newly recovered reminiscences about Schubert by his forgotten friend, the composer Joseph Lanz. *Music and Letters* 88, no. 2: 226–65.

Stokes, Richard. 2005. *The Book of Lieder: The Original Text of Over 1000 Songs.* London: Faber and Faber.

Wechsberg, Joseph. 1977. *Schubert: His Life, His Work, His Time.* New York: Rizzoli.

Weiler, Liesa Josephine. 2005. *Auf den Spuren Franz Schuberts in Steyr.* Vienna: Richard Funder.

Whitton, Kenneth S. 1981. *Dietrich Fischer-Dieskau, Mastersinger.* New York: Holmes and Meier.

————. 1999. *Goethe and Schubert: The Unseen Bond.* Portland, Oregon: Amadeus Press.

————. 1984. *Lieder: An Introduction to German Song.* London: Franklin Watts.

Youens, Susan. 1991. *Retracing a Winter's Journey: Schubert's* Winterreise. Ithaca, New York: Cornell University Press.

————. 1997. Schubert and his poets: issues and conundrums. In *The Cambridge Companion to Schubert.* Ed. Christopher Gibbs. Cambridge: Cambridge University Press. 99–120.

————. 1992. *Schubert:* Die Schöne Müllerin. Cambridge: Cambridge University Press.

————. 1997. *Schubert, Müller, and* Die Schöne Müllerin. Cambridge: Cambridge University Press.

————. 2002. *Schubert's Late Lieder: Beyond the Song Cycles.* Cambridge: Cambridge University Press.

————. 1996. *Schubert's Poets and the Making of Lieder.* Cambridge: Cambridge University Press.

Index of Schubert Songs

Poets' names appear in parentheses whenever more than one Schubert song shares the same title.

CD Track Listing

1. "Gretchen am Spinnrade"
   Ruth Ziesak, soprano, and Ulrich Eisenlohr, piano
   CD 8.554666

2. "Erlkönig"
   Johannes Kalpers, tenor, and Burkhard Kehring, piano
   CD 8.554667

3. "Suleika I"
   Ruth Ziesak, soprano, and Ulrich Eisenlohr, piano
   CD 8.554666

4. "Der Musensohn"
   Johannes Kalpers, tenor, and Burkhard Kehring, piano
   CD 8.554667

5. "Gruppe aus dem Tartarus"
   Regina Jakobi, mezzo-soprano, and Ulrich Eisenlohr, piano
   CD 8.554741

6. "Der Tod und das Mädchen"
   Wolfgang Holzmair, baritone, and Ulrich Eisenlohr, fortepiano
   CD 8.557568

7. "Der Wanderer"
   Hanno Müller-Brachmann, bass-baritone, and Ulrich Eisenlohr, piano
   CD 8.5555780

8. "Dass sie hier gewesen"
Julia Borchert, soprano, and Ulrich Eisenlohr, piano
CD 8.554797

9. "Auf dem Wasser zu singen"
Wolfgang Holzmair, baritone, and Ulrich Eisenlohr, fortepiano
CD 8.557568

10. "Der Einsame"
Hanno Müller-Brachmann, bass-baritone, and Ulrich Eisenlohr, piano
CD 8.5555780

11. "Im Abendrot"
Hanno Müller-Brachmann, bass-baritone, and Ulrich Eisenlohr, piano
CD 8.5555780

12. "Auflösung"
Christiane Iven, mezzo-soprano, and Burkhard Kehring, piano
CD 8.554739

13. "Lied eines Schiffers an die Dioskuren"
Cornelius Hauptmann, bass, and Stefan Laux, piano
CD 8.554738

14. "Die junge Nonne"
Julia Borchert, soprano, and Ulrich Eisenlohr, piano
CD 8.554797

15. "Wohin?" (from *Die Schöne Müllerin*)
Christian Elsner, tenor, and Ulrich Eisenlohr, piano
CD 8.554664

16. "Trockne Blumen" (from *Die Schöne Müllerin*)
Christian Elsner, tenor, and Ulrich Eisenlohr, piano
CD 8.554664

17. "Der Lindenbaum" (from *Winterreise*)
Roman Trekel, baritone, and Ulrich Eisenlohr, piano
CD 8.554471

18. "Der Leiermann" (from *Winterreise*)
Roman Trekel, baritone, and Ulrich Eisenlohr, piano
CD 8.554471

19. "Ständchen" (Rellstab, from *Schwanengesang*)
Michael Volle, baritone, and Ulrich Eisenlohr, piano
CD 8.554663

20. "Der Doppelgänger" (from *Schwanengesang*)
Michael Volle, baritone, and Ulrich Eisenlohr, piano
CD 8.554663

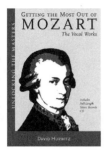

UNLOCKING THE MASTERS

The highly acclaimed Unlocking the Masters series brings readers into the world of the greatest composers and their music. All books come with CDs that have tracks taken from the world's foremost libraries of recorded classics, bringing the music to life.

"With infectious enthusiasm and keen insight, the Unlocking the Masters series succeeds in opening our eyes, ears, hearts, and minds to the great composers." – *Strings*

BEETHOVEN'S SYMPHONIES:
A LISTENER'S GUIDE
by John Bell Young
US $22.95 • 978-1-57467-169-8 • HL00331951

BRAHMS: A LISTENER'S GUIDE
by John Bell Young
US $22.95 • 978-1-57467-171-1• HL00331974

CHOPIN: A LISTENER'S GUIDE TO THE
MASTER OF THE PIANO
by Victor Lederer
US $22.95 • 978-1-57467-148-3 • HL00331699

DEBUSSY: THE QUIET REVOLUTIONARY
by Victor Lederer
US $22.95 • 978-1-57467-153-7 • HL00331743

DVOŘÁK: ROMANTIC MUSIC'S
MOST VERSATILE GENIUS
by David Hurwitz
US $27.95 • 978-1-57467-107-0 • HL00331662

THE GREAT INSTRUMENTAL WORKS
by M. Owen Lee
US $27.95 • 978-1-57467-117-9 • HL00331672

EXPLORING HAYDN: A LISTENER'S GUIDE
TO MUSIC'S BOLDEST INNOVATOR
by David Hurwitz
US $27.95 • 978-1-57467-116-2 • HL00331671

LISZT: A LISTENER'S GUIDE
by John Bell Young
US $22.99 • 978-1-57467-170-4 • HL00331952

THE MAHLER SYMPHONIES:
AN OWNER'S MANUAL
by David Hurwitz
US $22.95 • 978-1-57467-099-8 • HL00331650

OPERA'S FIRST MASTER: THE MUSICAL
DRAMAS OF CLAUDIO MONTEVERDI
by Mark Ringer
US $29.95 • 978-1-57467-110-0 • HL00331665

GETTING THE MOST OUT OF MOZART:
THE VOCAL WORKS
by David Hurwitz
US $22.95 • 978-1-57467-106-3 • HL00331661

GETTING THE MOST OUT OF MOZART:
THE INSTRUMENTAL WORKS
by David Hurwitz
US $22.95 • 978-1-57467-096-7 • HL00331648

PUCCINI: A LISTENER'S GUIDE
by John Bell Young
US $22.95 • 978-1-57467-172-8 • HL00331975

SHOSTAKOVICH SYMPHONIES AND CONCERTOS:
AN OWNER'S MANUAL
by David Hurwitz
US $22.95 • 978-1-57467-131-5 • HL00331692

SIBELIUS, THE ORCHESTRAL WORKS:
AN OWNER'S MANUAL
by David Hurwitz
US $27.95 • 978-1-57467-149-0 • HL00331735

TCHAIKOVSKY: A LISTENER'S GUIDE
by Daniel Felsenfeld
US $27.95 • 978-1-57467-134-6 • HL00331697

DECODING WAGNER: AN INVITATION TO HIS
WORLD OF MUSIC DRAMA
by Thomas May
US $27.95 • 978-1-57467-097-4 • HL00331649

AMADEUS PRESS

www.amadeuspress.com
Prices and availability subject to change without notice.